from

Ladbroke Grove

to

Boreham Wood

by

Vic Rowntree

"What life was like for a young lad from war-torn London during the 1950s when he found a new home in rapidly growing Boreham Wood"

PUBLISHED BY ELSTREE & BOREHAM WOOD MUSEUM, 2011

First published by
Elstree and Boreham Wood Museum in 2011

Published by Elstree and Boreham Wood Museum
1 Drayton Road, Borehamwood
Hertfordshire WD6 2DA

www.elstree-museum.co.uk
email: office@elstree-museum.co.uk

ISBN 978-0-9565297-1-8

Printed and bound in the UK by

MPG-Books Group, Bodmin and King's Lynn

01553 764728

Acknowledgements

Like many locals I am very grateful that the *'Elstree and Borehamwood Museum'* is
here to care for the treasured records of the history of our town and I wish to thank the
volunteers for their help in creating this book.

A special thank you is also extended to my dear friend **Derek Allen** for giving me his
permission to use some of his old photographs of Boreham Wood in the 1950s. His work
has made a major contribution for the enhancement of this book.

My thanks are also extended to all the staff of the **Borehamwood Library** who have given
me much of their time and assistance especially with my research on information on local
history.

I would also like to thank the following for their contributions: **Mrs. D.A. Purett**, Head
Teacher (Saffron Green School), **Margaret Young**, (Duty Planning Officer, Hertsmere
Borough Council), **Phil Attewell**, (Thornbury Gardens), **Mrs. Phoebe Davies**, (Nicoll
Way), **Veronica Males**, (High Canons). Members of the **Rowntree Family**, for all their
help, patience, support and understanding over the last three years of my involvement in
writing my book.

The following have kindly given their permission to reproduce their illustrations;

Boreham Wood Library
Derek Allen
Elstree & Boreham Wood Museum
Veronica Males

The contributors of illustrations and photos used in this book are shown against each picture.

Contents

Abbreviations of attributions for Illustrations and Photos. shown with Figure Numbers.

B.W.L.	Boreham Wood Library
D.A.	Derek Allen
E.B.W.M.	Elstree and Boreham Wood Museum
V.M.	Veronica Males
V.R.	Vic Rowntree
P.W.	Paul Welsh

INTRODUCTION

Having lived in Boreham Wood since 1952 I have seen many changes that have completely transformed the everyday lives of our older and younger residents living in this town.

This book is about what life was like for many families, including mine, who moved to Boreham Wood in the early 1950s. The government policy during that era was to build large numbers of publicly financed houses in satellite towns around London as a reaction to the housing shortages caused by enemy bombing and large amounts of substandard housing and overcrowding in the capital. Boreham Wood was chosen as a location where some of London's overspill could be relocated in a way that avoided ribbon-development. Thus many parts of the English countryside were turned into large housing estates to create new towns and homes. The village of Boreham Wood, which had already seen rapid expansion since the 1930s, became a town.

These criteria placed a huge responsibility on the government who had to negotiate with the farmers and land owners to use their land to build new houses, schools, shops, factories, churches, cinemas, libraries and other facilities that would be required by the local community.

Some of the best years of my life were during this era, growing up as a child and teenager in Boreham Wood in the 1950s. As you read through the chapters you may find something that triggers your own memories of the town in that decade.

Boreham Wood in the 1950s had so much to offer the new families and tenants who were coming to start new lives in the Hertfordshire countryside, where they could live and breathe clean fresh air instead of the dreadful **London Smog** they had endured for many years! I remember this time very well; it was such a lovely feeling moving into our brand new home. Everything was fresh, and the smell of wood and paint made me feel good!

This was only the beginning, There was more to come. We had so many new and exciting things to look forward to. As you read on, you will see exactly what I mean. It wasn't long before we discovered we were living in a mini **Hollywood** where we were surrounded by film studios and film sets. One that I shall never forget was the medieval castle built by the M.G.M. Studios for the film **Ivanhoe** which was made in 1952, starring Robert Taylor and Elizabeth Taylor.

We shall be looking at this and many other interesting items associated with this era including housing, shopping, education, transport, entertainment, radio, cinema, television, advertising and employment.

There were landmarks such as the **Thatched Barn** which had a very attractive **oldie-worldie** charm to it. Built in the 1930s in a typical Tudor style, it featured a beautiful thatched roof. It was a building that would certainly catch your eye when driving along the A1 Barnet By-Pass. It's sad that so many of our local landmarks are no longer with us and the remaining ones are gradually disappearing.

You may notice that I spell the name of this town **Boreham Wood** instead of the single-worded form **Borehamwood**. The two-worded form was historically the most common name for the wooded area near Theobald Street hamlet. When Boreham Wood was subjected to a massive post-war expansion, the new residents called for the **Elstree Station** to be renamed to include **Boreham Wood**. The residents' wish was granted in 1953 when the station was renamed **Elstree & Borehamwood**. Newcomers may have started using the one-word version after the station's title. Some also say that a local newspaper confirmed use of the one-word version in 1972 when it changed its name to the *Borehamwood & Elstree Post*.

Finally I hope you will enjoy reading my book as much as I have enjoyed writing it.

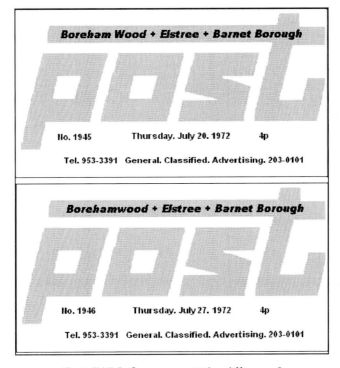

Fig 1. [V.R.] Can you spot the difference?

Cover: Jim Read, greengrocer and fruiterer,
with a customer on the pavement outside his shop in Shenley Road.

Artist's impression of Number 52 Red London Routemaster Bus
turning into Furzehill Road after servicing
at the Aldenham Garage.

Fig 2. [V.R.]

Vic, Marga and Charles Rowntree, 1946

Myself, Mum and Dad

Part One

Vic's Story

Fig 3. [V.R.]

Vic Rowntree outside 35 Lonsdale Road, 1952

LADBROKE GROVE

My parents lived in the Paddington and Kensington boroughs of the West End of London. In 1949 our home was at 35 Lonsdale Road, Ladbroke Grove W11 near the famous Portobello Road.

35 Lonsdale Road
in 2008.

Fig 4. [V.R.]

We lived in a downstairs basement flat commonly known as a **bed-sit**, which consisted of just one room that was used as a sitting room and bedroom and one very small kitchen which had no space for a table or chairs.

The toilet was situated in the back yard in a brick-built shed; this was where we had to go, come rain or shine! There was no bathroom; we used a tin bath filled with hot water in the sitting room.

Gas lighting consisted of a wall-mounted brass fitting, which had a small tap that we had to turn to let the gas through; we would then use a match to light it.

Entrance to the basement flat
35, Lonsdale Road
in 2008

Fig 5. [V.R.]

The living accommodation was very damp and unhealthy and due to my poor health, we were put on the 1950s L.C.C.'s priority housing list.

My First School - Colville Primary

The first school I attended in London was Colville Primary School in Lonsdale Road, Ladbroke Grove. This must have been between 1951 and 1952, because we moved to Boreham Wood in October 1952 when I was only six years old.

I don't remember much about Colville Primary School, only that it wasn't very far to walk from where we lived in Lonsdale Road, being in the same road. I especially remember the school dinners.

Opened in 1879, the school was a large commanding building standing just off the Portobello Road and is now regarded as an excellent architectural example of schools built by the old School Board of London when education was being greatly expanded.

The boys' entrance
Colville Primary School

2008.

Fig 6. [V.R.]

Colville Primary School
Lonsdale Road

2008

Fig 7. [V.R.]

BOREHAM WOOD

1 Knebworth Path

After six years of living in West London the day finally came in 1952 when we were offered a brand new three-bedroom council house in Boreham Wood just north of London in Hertfordshire.

Original records show and confirm that our house was part of **Block 206**, the plans for which were first submitted to the **Elstree Rural District Council** on the 19th February 1951 and approved on the 26th April 1951.

We were very lucky because our new house had three bedrooms, a bathroom and toilet, sitting room, kitchen and downstairs toilet. What a contrast in luxury to our old home!

The commencement date for building the house was the 20th July 1951 and the contractors were Gee, Walker and Slater Ltd. The final inspection and completion certificate illustrated on the next page was issued on the 19th November 1952. We actually moved in a month sooner!

One of our new neighbours **Phoebe**, then known as **Mrs. Knapp**, who was also moving on the same day into her new home at No.3 Knebworth Path, told me she remembers that day very well. She said *"Your family only had a small van and you never had any furniture. In fact, you only had your clothes, some suitcases and a couple of chairs!"*

It's funny, but I can remember to this very day, that it was a lovely feeling moving into our new home, the sun was shining and everything around me seemed to have a certain smell of *newness*. I suppose the fresh country air had something to do with it.

When we arrived the roads and pavements hadn't been completed. All around it was very muddy because there was still much building work going on. The houses opposite ours were unoccupied because the builders, who were working on them, were on strike!

Mother at the door of 1 Knebworth Path in 1959   Fig 8. [V.R.]

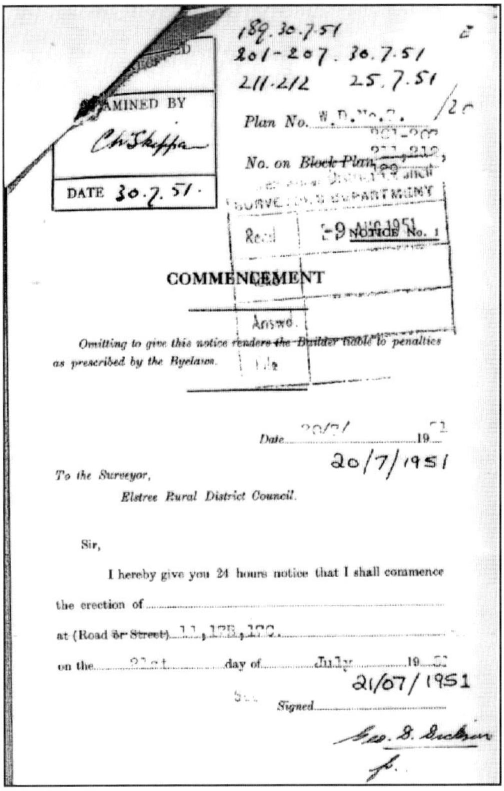

189. 30.7.51
201-207. 30.7.51
211-212 25.7.51

EXAMINED BY

DATE 30.7.51.

Plan No. W.D.No.7. /20

No. on ~~Block Plan~~

SURVEYOR'S DEPARTMENT

Rec'd -9 AUG 1951 NOTICE No. 1

Answd.

COMMENCEMENT

Omitting to give this notice renders the ~~Builder liable~~ to penalties as prescribed by the Byelaws.

Date 20/7/ 1951

20/7/1951

To the Surveyor,

Elstree Rural District Council.

Sir,

I hereby give you 24 hours notice that I shall commence

the erection of

at (Road ~~or Street~~)

on the 21st day of July 1951

21/07/1951

Signed

A copy of the certificate for the commencement date, 20th July 1951 for the building of 1, 3 & 5 Knebworth Path and 22 Nicoll Way.

Fig 9. [V.R.]

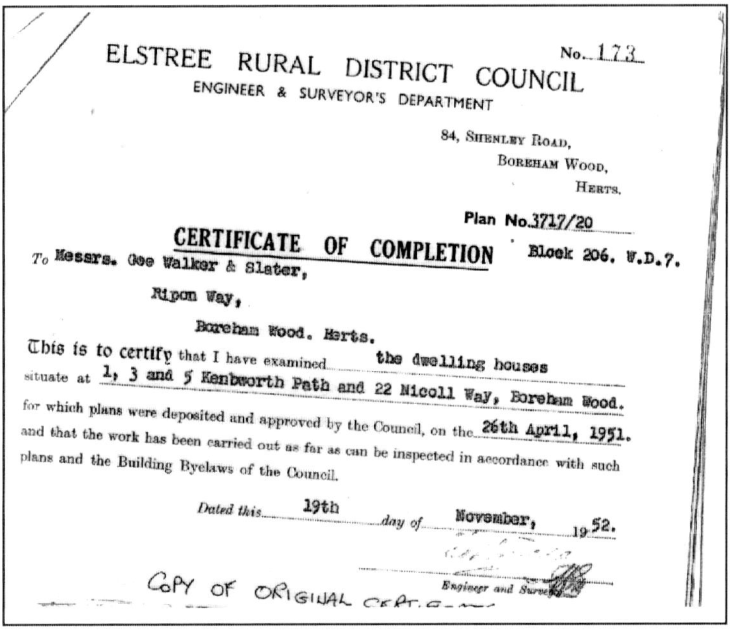

ELSTREE RURAL DISTRICT COUNCIL No. 173

ENGINEER & SURVEYOR'S DEPARTMENT

84, Shenley Road,
Boreham Wood,
Herts.

Plan No. 3717/20

CERTIFICATE OF COMPLETION Block 206. W.D.7.

To Messrs. Gee Walker & Slater,

Ripon Way,

Boreham Wood. Herts.

This is to certify that I have examined the dwelling houses situate at 1, 3 and 5 Kenbworth Path and 22 Nicoll Way, Boreham Wood. for which plans were deposited and approved by the Council, on the 26th April, 1951. and that the work has been carried out as far as can be inspected in accordance with such plans and the Building Byelaws of the Council.

Dated this 19th *day of* November, 1952.

Engineer and Surveyor

COPY OF ORIGINAL CERT.

A copy of the certificate for the completion date 19th November 1952 for 1, 3, & 5 Knebworth Path and 22 Nicoll Way.

Fig 10. [V.R.]

Fig 11. [V.R.] - Street Layout of LCC No 2 Estate Boreham Wood

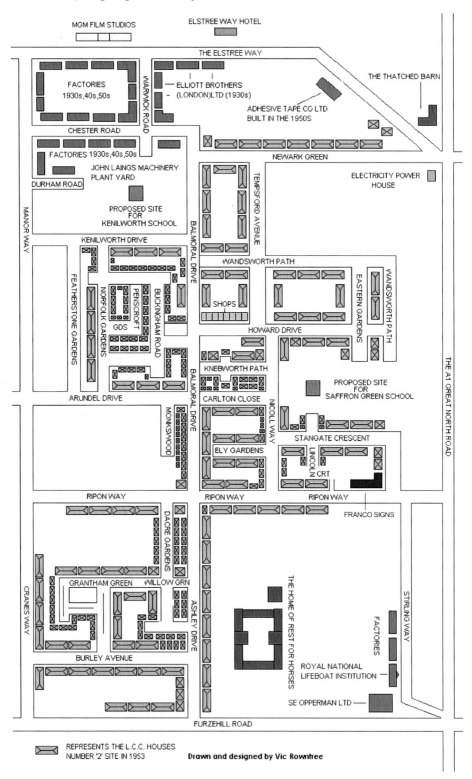

MGM FILM STUDIOS

ELSTREE WAY HOTEL

THE ELSTREE WAY

THE THATCHED BARN

FACTORIES
1930s,40s,50s

WARWICK ROAD

ELLIOTT BROTHERS
(LONDON)LTD (1930s)

ADHESIVE TAPE CO LTD
BUILT IN THE 1950S

CHESTER ROAD

NEWARK GREEN

FACTORIES 1930s,40s,50s

JOHN LAINGS MACHINERY
PLANT YARD

DURHAM ROAD

ELECTRICITY POWER
HOUSE

PROPOSED SITE
FOR
KENILWORTH SCHOOL

MANOR WAY

KENILWORTH DRIVE

TEMPSFORD AVENUE

WANDSWORTH PATH

FEATHERSTONE GARDENS

NORFOLK GARDENS

PENSCROFT

BUCKINGHAM ROAD

GDS

SHOPS

EASTERN GARDENS

WANDSWORTH PATH

BALMORAL DRIVE

HOWARD DRIVE

KNEBWORTH PATH

ARUNDEL DRIVE

BALMORAL DRIVE

CARLTON CLOSE

NICOLL WAY

PROPOSED SITE
FOR
SAFFRON GREEN SCHOOL

MONKSWOOD

ELY GARDENS

STANGATE CRESCENT

LINCOLN CRT

THE A1 GREAT NORTH ROAD

RIPON WAY

RIPON WAY

RIPON WAY

FRANCO SIGNS

DACRE GARDENS

CRANES WAY

GRANTHAM GREEN

WILLOW GRN

ASHLEY DRIVE

THE HOME OF REST FOR HORSES

STIRLING WAY

FACTORIES

BURLEY AVENUE

ROYAL NATIONAL
LIFEBOAT INSTITUTION

SE OPPERMAN LTD

FURZEHILL ROAD

REPRESENTS THE L.C.C. HOUSES
NUMBER '2' SITE IN 1953

Drawn and designed by Vic Rowntree

12

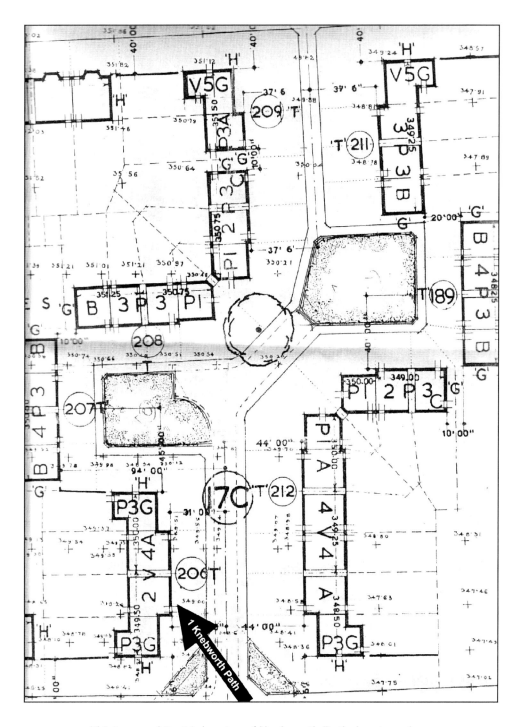

This is an architects' drawing of Knebworth Path showing where
our house, number '1' was to be built on plot 206 in section 2 V 4A.

Fig 12. [V.R.]

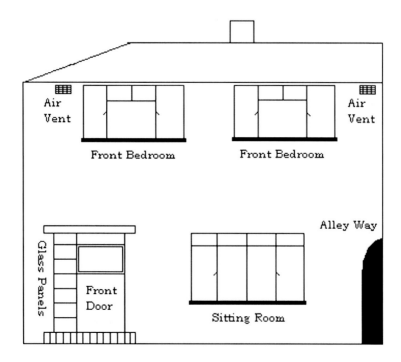

Fig 13. [V.R.] Front View of 1 Knebworth Path

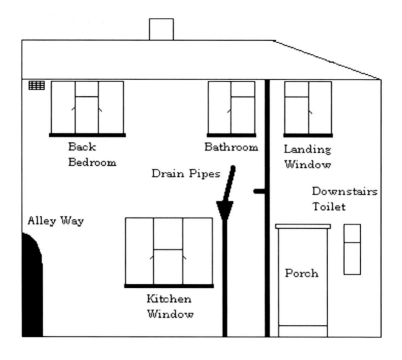

Fig 14. [V.R.] Rear View of 1 Knebworth Path

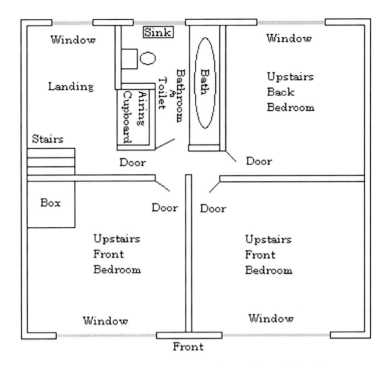

Fig 15. [V.R.] Upstairs Plan of 1 Knebworth Path

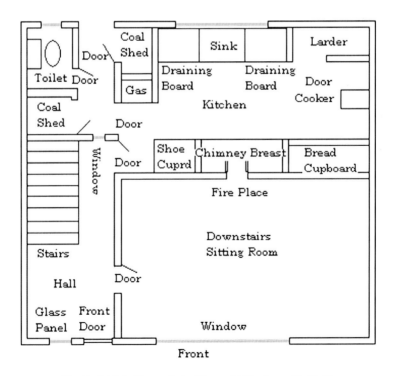

Fig 16. [V.R.] Downstairs Plan of 1 Knebworth Path

Problems with the New Estate

There were some very important issues in the early days of the L.C.C. No 2 Estate, concerning shops, schools and transport. Prompt action was needed due to lack of shops on the new housing estates; plans and locations for the buildings still had to be decided and approved by the local housing authorities.

The nearest shops that were around at the time were in Shenley Road, which soon became known to newcomers as *The Village*, as it was called by the original locals.

At the time there was only one bus running near our home and as it wasn't running regularly enough it caused a lot of inconvenience for the new tenants.

The lack of a reliable transport service meant many housewives had to walk to the Village to do their daily or weekly shopping. This was about a mile away from where they lived. On some days, especially during the winter months, the unfinished roads and pavements became almost impossible to walk on because of all the hazardous conditions.

The transport situation became a very important concern for the local authorities as many of the new residents had drawn up and signed a petition demanding a better bus service for Boreham Wood.

The heavy rains and dark evenings accentuated the problems for the new residents of Boreham Wood, especially those on the L.C.C.'s No.2 housing estate in Ripon Way. They said they had to walk along clay-covered, half made-up roads, which had been made messy by the building contractors working on the new housing estates.

Although the rain had made the roads an awful mess, it was much better when the weather was dry but even then the amount of dust that found its way into the new houses made it difficult to keep them clean.

If residents went by bus they had to walk to the nearest bus stop in Ripon Way where the bus fare was 3d (1.5p) to travel to the Village and 3d (1.5p) to return. Prices were in our old money, *pounds, shillings and pence, £.s.d.* In 1971 the Nation converted to the decimal system that we use today.

When they returned and stepped off the bus they also had to negotiate obstacles in the roads. Carrying heavy shopping baskets was not easy, especially during dark evenings because there was no street lighting. The installation of lamp posts and lighting was scheduled to take place only when the houses and roads had been completed.

Not all the new inhabitants were concerned about the absence of local shops in the area. but some deplored the long journey to the shops in Shenley Road several times a week, and were quite happy that many of the tradesmen actually called and delivered their orders directly to their homes.

All tenants agreed their difficulties in getting about, even in fine weather, were made worse by rain. One resident said "With all this building still going on, the road surface becomes coated with a slippery film of clay which makes walking awkward."

Conditions were worsened because pavements had not been laid in many places and stones, bricks and other building materials in the gardens made gardening very hard work.

The concerns about where the tenants of the new L.C.C. Housing Estates would shop were expressed at an annual meeting of the Elstree and Boreham Wood and District Chamber of Commerce, where it was stated there were other bus routes. The 52, 107 and 306 ran by the estates and tenants could go to either Barnet or Watford to do their shopping. Members felt that every effort should be made to encourage newcomers to shop in Boreham Wood rather than outside the area.

Sooner or later something had to be done for the tenants on the new housing estates, they just couldn't carry on living in this situation. Many of them thought of their children and how it could affect them as they grew up in the town and had to travel to school.

Following many complaints about the lack of shops, negotiations finally got under way and decisions were needed about who was going to build the shops and where they were going to be. John Laing & Sons, who were a well-known local and established building contractor, eventually won the contract.

John Laing & Sons were asked to provide plans for the building of the shops in Manor Way, and to state how long it would take to complete them as the L.C.C.'s tenants' situation was getting worse. John Laing & Sons had already taken two years to prepare the plans. They said that it would take one year to complete the shops once the plans were finished, but by that time there would be hundreds, if not thousands more families making the long trudge down to the Village. At the time John Laing's Deputy Surveyor said they had had difficulty in getting staff and in several cases he had to put jobs to other architects.

The situation attracted many different types of new home delivery services such as a baker, greengrocer, milkman and coalman.

The baker **Bob Freestone** drove around in his little brown and cream van that had his name painted on the side panels. You could buy freshly baked white bread, Hovis and lovely crusty rolls. I shall never forget the aroma!. He also sold all kinds of cakes including jam doughnuts, cheese cakes, cream slices, chocolate eclairs and crumpets. We were only treated to the latter on Saturdays.

Bob would turn up every morning and park his van in our street. My mother and the neighbours would go out and queue up to buy his goods.

In the early 1950s prices were very different to today. A large white loaf would then cost you 2½d (1p) and a cake 3d (1.5p).

I can't remember much about the greengrocer delivering, but one of my mother's old next-door neighbours recently told me that she remembers there was a man with a horse and cart who later delivered by van.

We had the **Co-operative** deliver our daily milk. They first opened their new Dairy Distribution Depot in Theobald Street on 4th September 1955. They advertised they could deliver much earlier than their competitors, the **A1** and the **Express** who started trading in 1956.

In 1959 I got a job working for the Co-operative during school holidays.

Charrington's, a local coal merchants, delivered our coal. In those days few could afford to have central heating installed, so only rich people enjoyed this luxury.

Coal was delivered about every two or three weeks. I'm not quite sure how often throughout the year, but I can clearly remember this lorry pulling up outside our house, loaded and stacked up with sacks of coal; later it was coke. He always reminded me of a chimney sweep because his face was black and covered with coal dust.

He would lift a sack of coal onto his back and carry it down our alley way, around the back of our house and empty it into our coal shed. We had two sheds but we only used one of them. I can remember my mother instructing me to always count the number of sacks the coalman was carrying just to make sure that we were getting as much as we had ordered.

A coal lorry in 2007.

Fig 17. [V.R.]

A Coalman
Delivering coal in 2007

Fig 18. [V.R.]

While we were waiting for our own local shops to be built in **Howard Drive** we made use of the newly-built shops in **Manor Way** as a temporary measure. It took roughly ten minutes from where we lived to walk there.

Around this time few shops were open. If my memory serves me right, there was only a Post Office, a chemist and a baker which were considered a priority for the new Ripon Way estate.

One of our next door neighbours, **Phoebe**, who lived at number 3 Knebworth Path said she clearly remembered her father-in-law going to the Post Office to collect his old age pension. She said he always came home moaning and groaning about the mothers he saw hanging about outside, chatting and smoking cigarettes they had probably bought using the family allowance they had just been paid!

Phil Attewell, a very good friend of mine who lives near the Manor Way shops, said he clearly remembered the parade of shops he visited in the mid to late fifties, .

Starting from the top end we had

Martin's	Similar to the bottom Martin's but had a Post Office and slightly smaller range of goods
Chemist	
Tip-Top	Dry cleaners
Peark's	General Stores
Baker	In those days, we had to buy our hot cross buns fresh early in the day, before they sold out!
Greengrocer	
Hairdresser	Gents' barber one side, ladies' the other
The Co-op	Butchers and general stores. Phil told me that he could still remember his mum's **divvy number** (dividend) that gave a discount like today's loyalty schemes (900149)
Bishop's	General stores, where people did most of their weekly shopping – it had two checkouts
Dewhurst's	Butcher
Morlyn's	A split shop, one half was haberdashery, button and things, the other half was a clothes shop
Manor View	TV, radio, records etc.
Bell & Lloyd	Pet foods, fertiliser etc.
Manor Home Stores	
Launderette	
Diane	Dress shop
Martin's	Bottom end newsagent, sweets, toys
Greengrocer	
Fish & Chip shop	Also sold wet fish

These shops were built by the local building contractor John Laing's, not the L.C.C.'s contractor.

Top end of
Manor Way Shops
2008

Fig 19. [V.R.]

Nine shops were eventually finished in Howard Drive between 1953-1954.

Tilson's	Greengrocer
Taylor Brother's	Grocer
Martin's	Newsagent
Chemist	
Off-Licence	
Draper's	
Hardware Shop	
Mathew's	Butcher
Fish and Chip shop	

Howard Drive shops
in 2008

Fig 20. [V.R.]

Fish and Chips

Buy Fish Tomorrow!

I remember queuing up on a Friday night outside our local shop in Howard Drive.

My mother always used to write on a little piece of paper *"4 x small Rock & Chips, 4 x gherkins and a bottle of Tizer"*.

Fig 21. [V.R.]

Arriving at the fish shop the queue was normally quite long. Some nights the customers would be queuing outside the door. Fish was good, plentiful and cheap for many years after the war because fish stocks around our shores had had a chance to recover during wartime. Fish & Chips was, and today still is, the most popular and number one favourite take-away!

Apart from the lovely smell, it was always interesting standing in the queue waiting to be served. One would hear all sorts of chatting going on - all the local scandal!. As soon as I got my order, I would run home as fast as I could and we all sat down and got stuck in. Someone would say *"Pass the salt & vinegar please"* or *"Have you buttered the bread yet?"* or *"Have you put the kettle on?"*

The type of shop grouping in Howard Drive was repeated in many other areas including Leeming Road, Wycliffe Road, Hartforde Road, Aycliffe Road, Croxdale Road, Thirsk Road. All had similar shops to those in Howard Drive, but not all of them had a Fish and Chip shop.

Soon after the building of Howard Drive shops, between 1954 and 1955, they built the *Holy Cross Church* in Balmoral Drive.

Holy Cross Church, (H.C.C.)
Balmoral Drive
in 2008

Fig 22. [V.R.]

In February 1957 a new pub called *The Suffolk Punch* was opened in Howard Drive. It belonged to the brewers *Charing & Co.* and stood directly opposite the shops.

The Suffolk Punch (S. P. P. H.) in Howard Drive

Fig 23. [V.R.]

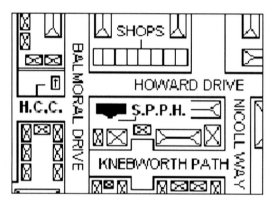

Detailed street map of the location of Howard Drive shops, church and pub

Fig 24. [V.R.]

Sometime afterwards big improvements were made to the long outstanding transport problems by the introduction of additional bus routes.

In 1953 the red number *52 London Transport bus* continued to run from Notting Hill Gate near Ladbroke Grove, Willesden, Neasdon, Kingsbury, Burnt Oak and terminated at Drayton Road in Boreham Wood.

It ran along the A1 Barnet By-Pass to Stirling Corner, turned left into Furzehill Road, turned right into Cranes Way, down to Ripon Way, junction with Manor Way, carried on straight down Manor Way, turned left into the Elstree Way, down to Shenley Road, turned left into Furzehill Road, turned right into Brownlow Road, turned right into Drayton Road and stopped. The return route was the same except the bus would turn right at the end of the road into Shenley Road and back up to the A1 and then head back to London.

No 52 Bus

Fig 25. [V.R.]

The number *52 bus* continued to run for many years but was eventually replaced with the *292* as we know it today. But it does not go to Notting Hill Gate.

Another red bus, the *107,* ran from Ponders End to Boreham Wood, travelling from Ponders End to Enfield, Oakwood, Barnet, Arkley, and terminating at Drayton Road.

The *141* bus ran from Edgware to Boreham Wood and terminated at the **Elstree Way Hotel**. On the 3rd February 1954 it was withdrawn and Route *107* was extended along the *141* route to Edgware Station and then onto Queensbury. Today it runs from Edgware to Barnet and not to Ponders End.

The *306*, a green bus, ran from Barnet to Boreham Wood, Watford and then terminated at Garston. Other buses running through Boreham Wood were the *355 **and** 358* to St. Albans; all were double-deckers, except the *355*.

Buses had a conductor to help passengers and collect fares. Differently coloured punch-tickets were pre-printed with the names of places where the bus stopped. The fare was printed in large letters on the ticket; the conductor punched a hole against the stop where the passenger boarded. An inspector checked tickets to ensure passengers had paid the correct fare and had not gone too far. In those days the bus drivers used to wear *white summer peaked caps!*

Although Boreham Wood had made improvements to its transport services, many people still preferred to shop locally or make that exciting trip down to the Village. The reason for this will become apparent.

Right - 107 Bus Tickets

Right - 141 Bus Tickets

Fig 26. [E.B.W.M.] Local Bus Signs and Tickets of the 1950s

KEEP YOUR MONEY CIRCULATING IN YOUR OWN DISTRICT IT WILL PAY YOU TO PAY A VISIT TO BOREHAM WOOD'S NEW SHOPPING CENTRE. HARTFORDE ROAD, COWLEY HILL ESTATE GET PERSONAL ATTENTION FROM THE PRIVATE TRADERS. ALL YOUR NEEDS CATERED FOR *ISSUED BY HARTFORDE ROAD TRADERS*	HARTFORDE ROAD TRADERS **COWLEY FISHERIES** WET, DRIED & FRIED FISH ---- DAILY ---- DIRECT FROM COAST One Quality Only..... THE BEST
BREN'S LTD. BUY YOUR GOODS LOCALLY ROLLERS, LAWN MOWERS, SEEDS, EVERYTHING FOR THE KITCHEN NUTS, BOLTS, SCREWS, CURTAIN WIRE & TRACKS, SIZE, PASTE, PAINT, and VARNISH & DISTEMPER. LINO, PYREX, CROCKERY & GLASSWARE, TOOLS, GLASS, HARDBOARD, SOLES, & HEELS, MATS, DON'T DELAY COME TODAY 107 HARTFORDE ROAD., BOREHAM WOOD Phone: Elstree 117 Issued by Hartforde Traders Association	**HARTFORDE ROAD TRADERS ASSOCIATION** SOMEONE'S BIRTHDAY!! *Is it yours NEXT WEEK?* IF SO CELEBRATE WITH A FIRST CLASS CAKE MADE WITH THE FINEST INGREDIENTS SPECIAL MIXINGS FOR THE KIDDIES DROP IN AND PLACE ORDER AT;- WILLIAMS BAKERY Personal Attention given. 105 HARTFORDE ROAD (L. Williams, Prop.) BOREHAM WOOD
BEST LINCOLNSHIRE POTATOES Direct from the farm to your door 16/- per cwt. 1/- deposit on bag Well below controlled Price **HOWARD'S** FRUITERERS AND GREENGROCERS 103 HARTFORDE RD., BOREHAM WOOD ELS 2656 ***and at 24 GREENHILL PARADE, BARNET*** BAR 3879 Issued by Hartforde Road Traders Association	H. ATTWELL THE MODERN BUTCHER 101 Hartforde Road, Boreham Wood Phone – ELS 3171 PERSONAL ATTENTION ALL FOODSTUFFS DISPLAYED IN MODERN REFRIGERATED SHOW CASE (FIRST IN BOREHAM WOOD) FREE FROM DUST, DIRT, HEAT AND FLIES NEW REGISTRATIONS WELCOMED Issued by Hartforde Road Traders Association
GEARY'S NEWSAGENTS, TOBACCONISTS, CONFECTIONERS SUB POST OFFICE 97 Hartforde Road, Boreham Wood WALLS ICE CREAM – TRI-ANG TOYS PAPERS DELIVERED Phone – ELSTREE 2338 Issued by Hartforde Road, Traders Association	**L. HURST (Chemist) LTD.** YOUR PRIVATE CHEMIST 95 HARTFORDE RD., BOREHAM WOOD PHONE: ELS 2600 All Sickroom and Nursery requirements Yardley, Max Factor, Morny, Ponds and Cosmetics Films Developed and Printed National Health Service Prescriptions Dispensed Issued by Hartforde Road Traders Association

Fig 27. [V.R.] Examples of advertisements for the shops in Hartforde Road in the Boreham Wood and Elstree Post in 1952

Going down *The Village* - Join me on a bus-ride!

As I've said, when we first arrived in Boreham Wood in 1952, there were no local shops near our house. The nearest were in Shenley Road which became known to everyone as *The Village*. There were other towns where we could go like **Barnet, Burnt Oak, Edgware, St. Albans** and **Watford**, but to get there involved travelling by public transport.

I can remember going down to the Village with my mother. Our journey began when we boarded a double-decker bus that was waiting for us at a temporary bus stop in Ripon Way. It has been difficult for me to identify the actual number of this particular bus, however I was advised by a member of the Elstree and Borehamwood Museum that it could have been just a temporary service laid on by the local council and that it may have been hired.

Temporary Bus Stop
near Ripon Way,
ahead the A1 Barnet By-Pass
(Great North Road)
Franco Signs Factory on the Left
c1950s.

Fig 28. [D.A.]

The A1 By-Pass facing South
Opperman's and the
Royal National Lifeboat Institution
on the right 1950s

Fig 29. [D.A.]

The bus was facing the A1 Barnet By-Pass, the Great North Road, where we turned left and then travelled north for about half-a-mile before a left turn at the cross-roads watching the sign for Boreham Wood. We travelled along the Elstree Way, passing on our right our first landmark, the *Thatched Barn*, which was demolished in 1989.

The Thatched Barn

Fig 30. [V.R.]

The A1 Cross-roads
c1950s

Fig 31. [D.A.]

On the left was the newly built factory of *Adhesive Tapes Ltd.*; built between 1950-1; immediately following this we had *Elliott Brothers (London) Ltd.*, who built some of the first computers and electronic defence equipment.

The Elstree Way, in the distance the Thatched Barn.

On the right, the building site and workman's huts for the new Adhesive Tapes Factory.

c1950s.

Fig 32. [D.A.].

One of Adhesive Tapes Factories in
Boreham Wood
Makers of *Sellotape*
1950s

Fig 33. [E.B.W.M.]

Sellotape was made in
Boreham Wood

Fig 34.
Sellotape Advertisement

Elliott's
First
Boreham Wood Factory
Elstree Way

Fig 35. [E.B.W.M.]

Elliott's
Experimental Computer
"Nicholas"

1952

Fig 36. [E.B.W.M.]

Continuing along this road there were some more factories and then over on the right stood the **Elstree Way Hotel**. In the early 1950s there was a bus terminus here.

The Elstree Way Hotel
c1950s.

Fig 37. [D.A.]

Moving on, next on the right we saw our second landmark, the white Clock Tower of the **M.G.M. Studios** and behind this the huge stages, which sadly are no longer with us. They were demolished in the 1980s and cold-storage warehouses replaced them.

M.G.M. Film Studios
with its
White Clock Tower
in the Elstree Way
c1950s

Fig 38. [D.A.]

There were some factories on the south side of the road forming part of Boreham Wood's industrial area. Continuing along the *Elstree Way*, just past M.G.M. there was a very large field and in the distance at the top of a mound there was a replica of a medieval castle, used quite regularly by the M.G.M. studios.

Ivanhoe's Castle

Fig 39. [E.B.W.M.]

On passing the Manor Way junction, looking to the left there was a little house that was surrounded by some trees and scrubs. My friend Phil Attewell recently told me that he remembers this house and said that one of the trees was a willow. The house and the trees were still there in the 1970s!

Elstree Way looking West towards Shenley Road from M.G.M. Studios, c1950
There was a considerable amount of open space at that time.
Fig 40. [P.W.]

We saw *Bullhead Road* on the left. It's worth mentioning that at this time the *petrol, fire and ambulance station, library, Venue and swimming pool* had not been built. In August 1955 the Boreham Wood & Elstree Post first mentioned commencement of work on a new *Police Station* to be built on part of the land in the Elstree Way. Continuing along, we came to *Maxwell Road* on the left where we saw the last of the industrial buildings used by the *London Adhesive Co. Ltd.*.

At the beginning of this road on the right-hand corner butting on to the Elstree Way, we had *Bullens Packing and Transportation Ltd*. As we passed this building, we came to the end of the Elstree Way, and the beginning of *Shenley Road*. There is a fork in the road spurring off from Shenley Road and heading in the direction of *Shenley*. In the centre of this fork there was a large brick reservoir standing on a piece of waste land which divided Shenley Road and the Elstree Way. This was for use by the fire brigade during the Second World War.

Looking east towards
the Elstree Way.
The building on the right is
Bullen's and directly opposite
on the left behind the sign is the
brick reservoir.
c1950s.

Fig 41. [D.A.]

Shenley Road Shops

Fig 42. [V.R.] Shenley Road Street Plan Early 1954

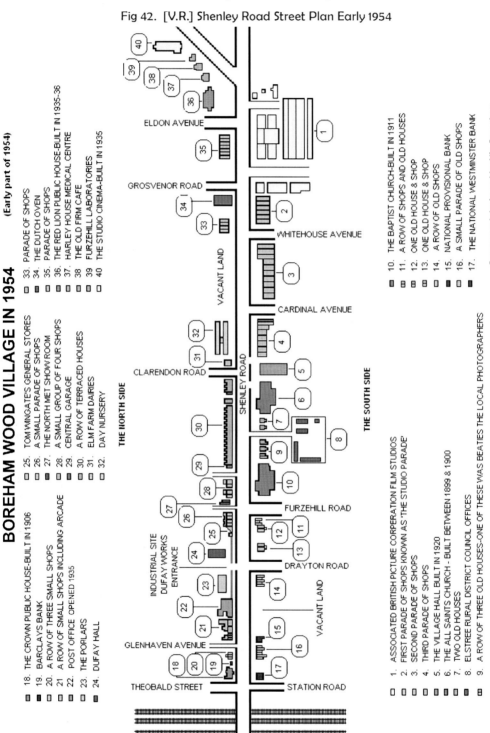

BOREHAM WOOD VILLAGE IN 1954

(Early part of 1954)

18. THE CROWN PUBLIC HOUSE-BUILT IN 1906
19. BARCLAYS BANK
20. A ROW OF THREE SMALL SHOPS
21. A ROW OF SMALL SHOPS INCLUDING ARCADE
22. POST OFFICE OPENED 1935
23. THE POPLARS
24. DUFAY HALL
25. TOM WINGATE'S GENERAL STORES
26. A SMALL PARADE OF SHOPS
27. THE NORTH MET SHOW ROOM
28. A SMALL GROUP OF FOUR SHOPS
29. CENTRAL GARAGE
30. A ROW OF TERRACED HOUSES
31. ELM FARM DAIRIES
32. DAY NURSERY
33. PARADE OF SHOPS
34. THE DUTCH OVEN
35. PARADE OF SHOPS
36. THE RED LION PUBLIC HOUSE-BUILT IN 1935-36
37. HARLEY HOUSE MEDICAL CENTRE
38. THE OLD FIRM CAFE
39. FURZEHILL LABORATORIES
40. THE STUDIO CINEMA-BUILT IN 1935

1. ASSOCIATED BRITISH PICTURE CORPERATION FILM STUDIOS
2. FIRST PARADE OF SHOPS KNOWN AS 'THE STUDIO PARADE'
3. SECOND PARADE OF SHOPS
4. THIRD PARADE OF SHOPS
5. THE VILLAGE HALL BUILT IN 1920
6. THE ALL SAINT'S CHURCH - BUILT BETWEEN 1899 & 1900
7. TWO OLD HOUSES
8. ELSTREE RURAL DISTRICT COUNCIL OFFICES
9. A ROW OF THREE OLD HOUSES-ONE OF THESE WAS BEATIES THE LOCAL PHOTOGRAPHERS
10. THE BAPTIST CHURCH-BUILT IN 1911
11. A ROW OF SHOPS AND OLD HOUSES
12. ONE OLD HOUSE & SHOP
13. ONE OLD HOUSE & SHOP
14. A ROW OF OLD SHOPS
15. NATIONAL PROVISIONAL BANK
16. A SMALL PARADE OF OLD SHOPS
17. THE NATIONAL WESTMINSTER BANK

Drawn and designed by Vic Rowntree

THE NORTH SIDE

THE SOUTH SIDE

ELDON AVENUE
GROSVENOR ROAD
WHITEHOUSE AVENUE
CARDINAL AVENUE
CLARENDON ROAD
FURZEHILL ROAD
DRAYTON ROAD
GLENHAVEN AVENUE
THEOBALD STREET
STATION ROAD
SHENLEY ROAD
VACANT LAND
INDUSTRIAL SITE DUFAY WORKS ENTRANCE
VACANT LAND

The Key Nos shown against the photos on the following
pages refer to the numbered items on this diagram

The bus finally reached the end of our journey at the stop outside the main entrance of the *Associated British Picture Corporation* (A.B.P.C.) studios. The film studio, as we knew it, no longer exists. A Tesco supermarket and petrol filling station now occupy most of the site.

We alighted from the bus at this point to continue on foot along Shenley Road for shopping. Our bus continued to its turning point in Drayton Road. We walked west along Shenley Road towards Elstree and Boreham Wood Railway Station.

Our walk, described in the following pages, is illustrated as far as possible with photographs taken about 1954 to provide an idea of the shops that existed during the 1950s.

Key No. 1
The Associated British
Picture Corporation
Film Studios
in Shenley Road.
c1950s.

Fig 43. [D.A.]

The following photo shows a No 107 bus finishing its journey in Drayton Road, early 1950s. The Dufay Hall and Hunt's Butchers are in the background.

107 Bus in Drayton Road - Early 1950s
Fig 44. [E.B.W.M.]

The South Side of Shenley Road

Built before WWII *Studio Parade* stretched from the A.B.P.C. Studios to Cardinal Avenue. The Grosvenor Hotel and Restaurant that served the film-making community stood on the corner nearest the studios. Tobacconists, newsagents and off-licences did good trade in the adjoining shops..

Key No 2.

The parade of shops after Elstree Studios was known as Studio Parade c1950s

Fig 45. [E.B.W.M.]

Crossing *Whitehouse Avenue* Studio Parade continued for a further 13 shops. Here could be had most everyday items. There was a baker, fishmonger, fruiterer, butcher, clothes stores, grocery, toyshop, hardware store, dry-cleaners and so on. Tesco's and Woolworth's were apparently attracted by their success and chose to open their first Boreham Wood outlets here in the 1950s.

Key No 3.

Studio Parade Whitehouse Avenue to Cardinal Avenue c1950s

Fig 46. [E.B.W.M.]

[E.B.W.M.] Panorama showing the buildings as they were in October 2011

Across *Cardinal Avenue*, we came to a small parade of 8 pre-war shops, before reaching the *Village Hall.* Boots the Chemist were located here with neighbours such as Bentley's Furniture Store, Meyer's Greengrocer, Payne's Florists, the Kiosk Tobacconist and Sainsbury's. Solicitors and Estate Agents came later. Taken in 1963, the photo shows traffic congestion had become a problem; the quiet village atmosphere was no more. Tesco's had replaced Woolworth's who moved to the opposite side of the road. The WWII Air Raid Siren and Police box were still to be seen. *All Saints' Church* was consecrated in 1910, the clock tower being added at the end of the 1950s.

Key No 4.

The shops between
Cardinal Avenue
and the Village Hall

1963

Fig 47. [E.B.W.M.]

Key No. 5

The Village Hall
in Shenley Road
in 2008.

Fig 48. [V.R.]

Key No. 6

The All Saints Church
in Shenley Road with its tower
in 2008.

Fig 49. [V.R.]

Panorama showing the buildings as they were in October 2011

Walking past the church there were some old houses, one of which was demolished in 1941 to make way for a service road which later became the entrance for the car park and offices of the *Elstree Rural District Council.*

Crossing this road there were more buildings; one, before the *Baptist Church,* was occupied by *Beattie's,* a local photographer. The Baptist Church site is now *Furzehill Parade.*

The Baptist Church stood in a field on the corner of Furzehill Road.

The hedge in Fig 51, and on the left of Fig 52. belonged to the Baptist Church.

Panorama showing the buildings as they were in October 2011

Across Furzehill Road was a row of three shops. The corner shop was Geo. Lilley's, who sold and repaired radios and televisions. The second shop was Kilby's, a grocer, the third shop was a Co-op, at one time also run by Cherry's followed by a semi-detached house one half of which was Byers, a confectionery shop that sold tobacco and toys.

Key No.11
George Lilley's shop
on the corner of
Furzehill Road and Shenley Road
c1950s.

Fig 52. [D.A.]

Key No .11 - 13
George Lilley's
Kilby's Provisions
Co-op shoes or Cherry's
Byers
c1950s.

Fig 53. [E.B.W.M.]

Following this group of shops and houses there was a gap about the width of a house at the end of which was *Hunt's the butcher's,* again part house and part shop. There was some vacant land upon which once stood a house that was a *Dolls' Hospital.*

Key No .12 - 13
Byers and Hunt's
Butchers
c1950s.

Fig 54. [E.B.W.M.]

Panorama showing the buildings as they were in October 2011

Across Drayton Road was a small block of four old shops, which still exist.

Key No. 14
A Parade of four shops
in Shenley Road
in 2008.

Fig 55. [V.R.]

Key No. 14
Wilkins Boots and Shoes

Fig 56. [E.B.W.M.]

Next came some vacant land, sometimes called the orchard. See Key 14-15 below

Key No. 14 - 15
Vacant Land, the Orchard,
decorated for the Coronation of
Her Majesty Queen Elizabeth II
June 1953

Photo on Dufaycolor Film made
in Boreham Wood

Fig 57. [E.B.W.M.]

Panorama showing the buildings as they were in October 2011

The National Provincial Bank stood at the end of the orchard. The same building also housed Thomas Hughes who was a local surveyor connected with much of the building being carried out in the area.

Key No. 15
The National Provincial Bank &
Thomas Hughes (Chartered Surveyors)
in 1954.

Fig 58. [B.W.L.]

Key No. 16

Station Parade
in 2008.

Fig 59. [V.R.]

Next, beyond the bank, stood Edwardian shops, Station Parade included, which contained *Elstree Radio, Groom's Menswear and Kidwell's Newsagents*. Finally the building at the end of the road was the *National Westminster Bank*. The curious building was converted to a *Turkish Restaurant* in 2010, having been used by a variety of businesses.

Key No. 17

National Westminster Bank.
Station Road
South-West Corner of the Village
2008

Fig 60. [V.R.]

Panorama showing the buildings as they were in October 2011

The North Side of Shenley Road

The *Crown Public House* commanded the view of the north-west corner of Shenley Road. It was built in 1906 by Clutterbuck & Co. a well known 19th and early 20th century brewing company based in Stanmore who owned several public houses and inns in Hertfordshire. This Edwardian public house was formerly named *The New Crown*, serving the old village of Boreham Wood, replacing the former *Crown Inn* located at 2 Theobald Street. Later the *New Crown* was named *The Crown Hotel*.

Key No. 18
The Crown Public House
Shenley Road
2008.

Fig 61. [V.R.]

Looking North along Theobald Street before the War Memorial was moved in the 1950s, one could see the original *Crown Inn* behind the memorial, and many of the oldest buildings in the area.

Key No. 18
Theobald Street and
The Crown Public House
Shenley Road

Fig 62. [E.B.W.M.]

In those days the station entrance was on the Elstree side of the bridge. The bridge was always a great place to stand for a little train-spotting, steam engines, of course!

A goods train coming from town.

1953

Fig 63. [E.B.W.M.]

Barclays Bank was a small building next to The Crown, close to the bus stop. When it became a newsagent's an extension was added to the upper part providing living accommodation, which considerably changed the building's appearance.

Key No. 19

Barclays Bank

Fig 64. [D.A.]

Key No. 20
A row of three shops built 1910

2008

Fig 65. [V.R.]

After the Bank we had a small group of shops built in 1910. *King's Fishmongers*, *Hastwell's Hardware* shop, later *Boreham Wood Ironmongers*. At the end of the row there was *Pressey's Drapers & Ladies' Clothes* shop.

Key No. 20
Boreham Wood Ironmongers,
formerly Hastwell's
c1956

Fig 66. [E.B.W.M.]

Panorama showing the buildings as they were in October 2011

Across *Glenhaven Avenue*, were three shops, firstly *E.J. Freestone's Bakers*, (now a Travel Agents) second, *Theobald Farm Dairies*, (now *Shenley Sandwich Bar*) and third, *Charrington's Fuel Merchants* (now financial services). Beyond these shops there was *Cyril Brine's* selling cycles and motor cycles. His store was followed by the *Shenley Road Market Arcade*.

Key No. 21
Freestone's Bakery,
Theobald Farm Dairy,
and Charrington's Fuel
c1950s

Fig 67. [E.B.W.M.]

Key No. 21
Shopping Arcade
c1950s

Fig 68. [E.B.W.M.]

After the Arcade came the *Boreham Wood Post Office* that was opened in 1935. It replaced the earlier post office that was situated in the row of shops on *Station Parade*. Although fairly typical of the design used by the Post Office, it indicates the social economic growth of Boreham Wood in the early 20th Century. Sadly, this building is no longer used as a Post Office; it was modified and used for training and employment.

Key No. 22
The Old Post Office
in the c1950s.

Fig 69. [D.A.]

Panorama showing the buildings as they were in October 2011

The Poplars, a large house, and the entrance to the *Dufay Works* were almost opposite Drayton Road. A large wall provided security for the site.

Key No. 23 - 24
The Poplars and Dufay Hall
1953

Fig 70. [D.A.]

Key No. 25
Tom Wingate's General Stores

late 1930s

Fig 71. [E.B.W.M.]

To the right side of Dufay's wall *Tom Wingate* had managed his General Store before the War. To entertain his customers he wore fancy dress. After Tom Wingate's there was another parade of old Shenley Road shops. Over the years the occupants of the premises have changed many times. The Co-op was the principal business.

Key No. 26

The Shenley Road Co-op
1949

Fig 72. [E.B.W.M.]

Panorama showing the buildings as they were in October 2011

The *North Met Show Room* was next to the Co-op.

Key No. 27

First the North Met Show Room and beyond, boarded up, the remaining derelict shops of the 1950s
2008

Fig 73. [V.R.]

Next was a group of four shops. An alley led to Laurel Cottages at the rear. The shops included Clinton's Gents' Hairdressers, Booth's Clothes, Read's Greengrocery and Hanson's Confectioners. In later years Hanson's sold the business to the Rudd family, but they kept the tea room and catering facility at the rear of the premises until the beginning of the 21st Century. Sadly their building was sold for redevelopment. Marks & Spencer's and Starbuck's and some other retail outlets, also occupied the new building.

Key No. 28

Left: Booth's Clothes
Centre: Jim Read's Greengrocery
Right: Hanson and Maud's Confectionery shop.
c1958

Fig 74. [E.B.W.M.]

A home-made ice-cream from Hanson's trolley was a real treat!

Key No. 28

Hanson's Ices

Fig 75. [E.B.W.M.]

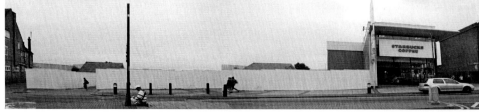

Panorama showing the site of demolished buildings in October 2011

The alley beside Hanson's led to the Keystone's Knitting Mills which made ladies' lingerie and stockings before they closed in the early 1950s.

The **Central Garage**, still serving the local community in the late 1960s, was across the alley.

Key No. 29

Central Garage

Fig 76. [E.B.W.M.]

After the Central Garage there was a long row of terraced houses that were pulled down in 1961 to make way for new shops including Fields and Sainsbury's Supermarket.

Key No. 30   Terraced Houses in Shenley Road
Fig 77.   [E.B.W.M.]

Key No. 30

Sainsbury's 1960s

Fig 78. [E.B.W.M.]

Panorama showing the buildings as they were in October 2011

At the end of the long row of houses we reached **Clarendon Road** and crossing over to the other side came **Elm Farm Dairies**.

Key No. 31
The Elm Farm Dairies
c1950s.
Notice the air-raid siren

Fig 79. [D.A.]

After the dairy was a large area of undeveloped land on which in 1942 they built a temporary building for use as a day nursery.

Key No. 32
The Day Nursery in Shenley Road c1950s.

Fig 80. [D.A.]

Next came a group of three shops that were standing practically on their own until more were added on both sides in the mid fifties The three shops were built just before WWII.

Key No. 33
The three original shops built before WWII.
More shops were added
on both sides in 1954 / 55.

2008

Fig 81. [V.R.]

Panorama showing the buildings as they were in October 2011

The last building before Grosvenor Road was the **Dutch Oven**, Ernest Freestone's (E.J.) bakery and restaurant, built 1934. There were three Freestone bakers in the area. E.J.'s brother Robert had bakeries in Boreham Wood, and the eldest brother Wheaton had one in Shenley. The Dutch Oven was sold shortly before E.J. died in 1952. The photo shows the building in its heyday and shows the gap in the buildings mentioned previously.

Key No. 34
The Dutch Oven was owned by
E.J. Freestone.

Fig 82. [E.B.W.M.]

Eventually Boreham Wood acquired a taste for spaghetti and the bakery-site hosted some Italian Restaurants: **The Gondola** and **Signor Baffi** and in 2010 **Benjamino's** have now departed. A clothes store and an estate agent have used the building, but the facade retains much of its character.

Key No. 34
The Dutch Oven was owned by
E.J. Freestone.

In 2008 it was Benjamino's
Italian Restaurant.

Fig 83. [V.R.]

Crossing to the other side of Grosvenor Road, the space on the corner was where E.J. kept chickens; a Barclays Bank was subsequently built there. After this came the very last parade of shops for this side of Shenley Road.

Key No. 35
The last parade of shops
on the north side of Shenley Road.

Fig 84. [V.R.]

Panorama showing the buildings as they were in October 2011

Next, after the shops came *Eldon Avenue*, with its late 1930s maisonettes. Shortly after the War pre-fabs were built at its north end for emergency housing.

The *Red Lion* public house, built in 1935-6 ceased as a pub in 1990. It was converted into a *McDonald's*.

Just past the pub stood *Harley House*, a large detached house that was a medical centre used by doctors and a dentist. Immediately after this was *The Old Firm Café*, half house and half shop. Next was *Furzehill Laboratories*, which was also partly a house.

Key No. 38 & 39
The Old Firm Café followed by Furzehill
Laboratories c1950s

Fig 86. [D.A.]

The last building in this part of Shenley Road was the *Studio Cinema* built in 1935,. When this area was redeveloped in the 1980s, the houses and cinema were replaced with modern offices.

Key No. 40

The Studio Cinema in the c1950s

Fig 87. [D.A.]

Panorama showing the buildings as they were in October 2011

Summary of Major Developments since 1954

Many new shops were built from 1954 onwards to meet the needs of the expanding town. All the vacant land on both sides of the high street was filled in, demolishing any obstructions in the process. Eventually, from the 1960s, old buildings were replaced by new ones. Some, such as the houses in Shenley Road and parts of the studio sites, had been part of the Village community for many years.

New Shops
Between Furzehill Road and Drayton Road.
built 1957-58

2008

Fig 88. [V.R.]

New Shops
Between Drayton Road and the National Provincial Bank
built 1955

2008

Fig 89. [V.R.]

New Shops:

The Poplars and Dufay Works entrance.
built 1957

2008

Fig 90. [V.R.]

New Shops

Clarendon Road to Grosvenor Road
late 1954-1955.

2008

Fig 91. [V.R.]

New Shops

Central Garage
to Clarendon Road

built c1961

Fig 92. [E.B.W.M.]

A more recent development involved the sale of most of the land occupied by Elstree Studios to Tesco's who built a supermarket where films were once made.

New Shops

Tesco Supermarket

built c1989

Fig 93. [E.B.W.M.]

Redundant buildings behind Shenley Road, once used for manufacturing by firms such as Wellington and Ward's and Keystones, were turned into the Boulevard 25 Shopping Centre. After a few years, under new ownership, it became Borehamwood Shopping Park. The trend away from small high street shops to these big stores has to do with the convenience provided by motor cars and being able to do all one's shopping in one place. The availability of parking close to the big stores is appreciated by motorists, while the difficulty of loading goods on the high street is not. The pressure on individual shops created by competition from the big companies has seen the demise of the old businesses. A consequence is that Shenley Road is now filled with charity shops, fast-food outlets, betting shops and estate agents.

New Shops

Borehamwood Shopping Park

built c1990

Fig 94. [E.B.W.M.]

Shopping Experiences

When we first moved to Boreham Wood in 1952 we were still using Ration Books issued by The Ministry of Food.

Fig 95.
Ministry of Food Advertisement in 1952

Despite the challenges of rationing, family diets contained more bread, vegetables and milk than children have today. The post-rationing years saw a steady increase in meat consumption, which only began to wane in the 1980s.

The 1950's diet was high in fat, however. Potatoes would probably have been roasted in saturated fat rather than today's healthier alternatives like unsaturated vegetable oil.

In celebration of the Queen's Coronation in 1953, everyone was allowed an extra 1lb of sugar and 4oz of margarine during the Coronation month.

Two years later rationing finally ended, with meat and bacon coming off the ration in June 1954. The 1950s saw a record number of families with young children, as the birth rate soared in the post-war baby boom.

After the war, when the soldiers came home, women had given up their jobs in factories and on farms, and women's magazines emphasised the value of their roles as housewives and homemakers. Mothers cooked fresh food; ready-meals and supermarkets had not been invented.

School dinners provided a hot meal at midday for just over half of all children in 1950, rising to a peak of 70% in 1966. As it had done during the war, the school meals service continued catering for children from all backgrounds and not just those from poor families. This service was regarded as a great success, producing healthier children and encouraging better behaviour, particularly when children and teachers ate together in small groups. School food was a typical 1950s fare; meat and two vegetables, macaroni cheese, fish on Fridays and always a cooked dessert such as rice pudding, semolina, tapioca or jam sponge and custard.

In 1955, commercial TV was launched and the new advertising jingles and slogans gradually became part of the culture.

Snap, crackle and pop, Go to work on an egg, and the first *Oxo* commercial, with its idealised nuclear family, made such an impression that they were selected as favourites by Channel 4 viewers nearly half a century later.

There was much less choice in the 1950s compared with today. Fresh fruit and vegetables were bought mainly from British growers, so people ate what was in season. Strawberries would be in the shops for just a few weeks in the summer and there were no fresh peas, beans or salad in winter. Bananas and oranges, which had virtually disappeared during the war, began to reappear.

Food was a major part of most families' spending, taking up about a third of the average income.

In Coronation year, shopping was a very different experience.

To get their rations, every household had to register with a butcher and a grocer.

We had to queue up at the counter, and what we took home depended on what they had in stock. The shop assistant would weigh or measure each item and wrap it in paper as most food was sold loose. Since few homes had fridges, people usually shopped for fresh food every day. Virtually all food was sold from small specialist shops and many people had their bread, milk, vegetables and groceries delivered.

But transformation of shopping began in this decade. With encouragement from the Government, which was worried by the shortage of labour, the bigger food retailers began to open self-service shops, an idea copied from the United States. As a customer entered the shop they were handed a wire basket or the precursor of the shopping trolley – a wheeled frame that would hold two baskets, known as the pram.

To the modern palate, 1950s food would seem bland and monotonous. More than a decade of rationing and food shortages meant that plain cooking was all that most housewives knew. With only 2oz of cheese and 5oz of bacon allowed a week for each person, cooks had to improvise. When the rationing ended people found freedom when doing everyday shopping.

"Where do we go?", "Where can we buy this?", "Where can we buy that"', "Where did you get that?' This was some of the typical jargon we would hear from many mums, dads and neighbours who were trying to get the best deals for their family budget.

In addition to *this word-of-mouth process*, advertising was used by many local traders who would often use the *Boreham Wood & Elstree Post* to advertise their goods. In May 1953 they charged 2d (less than 1p) per word to advertise!.

The local newspapers had their regulars, who advertised every week. The advertisements in those times were only printed in *black & white* which looked very plain and boring by today's standards.

THE DUTCH OVEN
195 - SHENLEY ROAD - BOREHAM WOOD
ANNOUNCING!
OUR SPECIAL LUNCH - 3 COURSES for 3/6
Served from 12 - 2.30 pm - All Xmas evening
Parties & Meetings Catered for 6 - 10 pm

Enquiries Invited

Advertisement in
Boreham Wood Post

Fig 96.

1956

HOT EELS & MASH
Mash and Liquor ---- Hot Pies
Your favourite dish from a quality fish shop
THURSDAY----FRIDAY----SATURDAY
RICHES & SONS
132 SHENLEY ROAD-BOREHAM WOOD

Advertising in Boreham
Wood Post

Fig 97.

1958

SHOPPING WITH PLEASURE
VISIT THE NEW
Self Service Establishment
144 Shenley Road, Boreham Wood
SERVE YOURSELF FROM OUR LARGE SELECTION OF
GROCERIES, FRESH FRUIT, BISCUITS, ETC., EVERY-
THING UNDER MODERN AND HYGIENIC CONDITIONS.
'SHOP WITH EASE AND BE PLEASED'
OUR MANAGER WILL BE PLEASED TO HELP YOU

Advertising the first
'Self-Service-Store'

Fig 98.

1958

ANNOUNCEMENT
For Boreham Wood & Surrounding Districts
S. HIRSH, of 4 Central Parade, Edgware
(ESTABLISHED IN THE CITY OF LONDON 1921), WILL
SHORTLY BE OPENING A HIGH CLASS LADIES
& GENTS TAILORING ESTABLISHMENT, INCLUDING
RIDING WEAR AT:—
201 SHENLEY ROAD
BOREHAM WOOD
Keep your eye on this advertisement for the Opening Date

Advertisement in
Boreham Wood Post

Fig 99.

1951

It's surprising how many shops advertised in the *Boreham Wood & Elstree Post* during the 1950s. The lists on the following pages give an idea of the shops that were trading around that time. Sadly, many of these shops have long since gone. I and many other locals in the town are constantly having discussions about what we used to have in the Village and our own personal memories that go with the different shops we remembered fondly.

The *Village feeling* has now completely gone! We used to have a traditional *Woolworths*, which first opened its doors on Friday 25th September 1953. It featured goods that could be purchased for minimal prices. It closed its doors for the very last time in 2009.

Shop Advertising

SHENLEY ROAD SHOPS 1950s
WHO ADVERTISED IN THE BOREHAM WOOD & ELSTREE POST

Year	Name of Shop	Retail or Trade
1950	Hill & Simmons	Bakers
1950s	Post Office	Post Office
1950-4	Hastwell's	Ironmongers
1950-9	Marianne	Ladies Knitwear & Wool
1951	Falcon Shoes	Shoe Shop
1951-2	Geo. D. Lilley	Radio. Television, Prams
1951-2	Victor Stores	Hardware & Domestic
1951-2	A. 1 Dairies (shop)	Milk and Dairy Products
1951-2	Cane	Confectionery, Toys, Tobacco
1951-2	Eve (Studio Parade)	Perfumery and toilet requisites
1951-2	Byers	Confectionery, Tobacco
1951-3	J.Sainsbury	Grocer
1951-8	L.Beattie	Photographer
1951-8	North Met	Electricity Show Room
1952	Desborough & Jane's Ltd	Newsagent, Stationery Tobacco
1952	Self Service	All in one shop
1952-8	Cyril Brine	Cycles and Motor Cycles
1952-8	Bob Freestones	Bakers
1952-8	S. Hirsch	High Class Ladies & Gents Clothes
1953	Kingston's	Butchers
1953	Living Stones	Greengrocer
1953-8	Shepherd's	Toys Shop (all makes)
1953	Maypole Dairy Co. Ltd	
1954	Kings	Fishmongers
1954	Barclays Bank	
1954	C. Pressey	Drapers
1954	The Arcade	Indoor market
1954	Tom Wingate	General Stores
1954	McNaughtion Chemist	Chemist
1954	Spot Café	Café
1954	Joanne	Hairdresser
1954	William's	Dentist
1954	Jean's	Ladies Outfitters
1954	Williams Butcher	Butcher
1954	Williams Brothers	Provisions
1954	Theobald Farm Dairy	Milk & Provisions
1954	Charrington's	Fuel Merchants
1954	Lloyds Bank	Bank
1954	Elm Farm Dairies	Dairy Products
1954	Hanson & Maud	Confectioners
1954	Central Garage	Car Sales, Service
1954	Molly's Café	Café
1954	Booths	Ladies Underwear
1954	J. E. Read	Greengrocer
1954	J. Mason	Auctioneers
1954-6	T.T.A.	Timer, Tools & Accessories
1954-8	R. Pratt	Gents Hair Dresses
1954-8	Rowland's	Newsagent-Confectionery
1954-9	London Co-operative Society	Groceries
1954-9	R.W. Bradshaw	Opticians & Microscopes
1954-9	Janes & Adams	Radio & Television
1954 -9	Daykins	Sowing Machines & Wool

	SHENLEY ROAD SHOPS 1950s	
	WHO ADVERTISED IN THE BOREHAM WOOD & ELSTREE POST	
Year	Name of Shop	Retail or Trade
1954 -9	Candies	Sweet Shop
1955	Achille Serre	Quality Cleaning
1955-6	Thomson's	Furnishers & Bedroom Suits
1956	Osbourne & Sons Ltd	Wines & Spirits
1956	Sydney Rumbelows	Radio & Television
1956	Contessa	Dresses & Fabrics
1956	Boreham Wood & Elstree Post	Local Newspaper
1956	Kingshill	Jewellers
1956	The Dutch Oven	Restaurant
1956-8	Girlings	Boys', Men's and Ladies' Wear
1956-8	E.G. Spiers Stores	Lawnmowers, timber, wood, paint,
1956-9	Riches & Sons	Fish & Chips & Pie & Mash
1957	Katherine Fashions	Ladies Clothes
1957	Home Decorators	DIY
1957	S.W. Thomson	Ice-Cream, Greeting Cards
1957-8	Mitchell's (Drapers)	Soft Furnishing,
1957-8	Ralph's	Shoe Shop
1957-8	Millers	Hair Dressers
1957-8	Faith Heath (opposite Post Office)	Prams, Cots, Highchairs, Toys
1957-8	Marber (then Blake's 1958)	Men's Wear
1957-8	Suzy	Hair Artist
1957-9	Byron Wine Stores	Free Off Licence
1958	Girlings	Boys & Men's Wear
1958	Myriad	Grocers
1958	Gordon's Garden	Garden Centre
1958	J.G. Sansom	Nurseryman & Florist
1958	Boreham Wood Ironmongers	Hardware
1958	Gordon's Garden	Garden Centre
1958	Benjamin (Chemist) Ltd	Chemist
1958	C & Q Self Service Store	Various Groceries
1958	Wilkins	Shoe Shop. Footwear
1958	Pauline Miller	School of Dancing
1958	Summers	Furnishers
1958	John Tyler's	Shoe Shop
1958	Bob Freestones	Baker
1958	Anne Chessell	Ladies, Children, Babies Wear
1958	F.J. Bunton	Suits, Blazers, Coats, Shirts
1958	Humming Bird	Motor Cycles, Scooters, Robin Reliant
1958	Jack Frusher	Turf Accountant
1958	S.H. Payne	Florist
1958	Woolwich Building Society	
1958	F.W. Woolworth	Sweets, Toys, Cloths, Hardware,
1958-9	Boots	
1958-9	London Co-operative Society	
1959	The Victoria Wine Company	Off Licence
1959	Tonibell Ice Cream	Café
1959	F.E. Pateman	Confectionery, Tobacco
1959	Howard Brothers	Clothes, Sports Wear
1959	B.B. Evans	Self Service Store
1959	Boots	
1959	F.W. Woolworth	New location

Earlier Shenley Road Shops 1920-1940

GUIDE SHEETS FOR EARLIER SHOPS AND THEIR LOCATIONS
SOUTH SIDE

Location	Name of Shop	Retail or Trade
British International Studios		
Studio Parade	The Grosvenor	Café
Studio Parade	R. Acason	Newsagent
Studio Parade	Eve	Hairdresser
Studio Parade	H Cleaver	Grocer / Sweet Shop
Studio Parade	J. Downe, Mr Cleaver	Grocer
Studio Parade	Osbornes	Off Licence
White House Avenue		
Studio Parade	Bob Freestone	Baker
Studio Parade	F. Archer, Garrard	Greengrocer
Studio Parade	Warner	Butcher
Studio Parade	Bond	Fishmonger
Cardinal Avenue		
Parade 8 shops	London Tobacconists Kiosk	Tobacconists
Parade 8 shops	J Sainsbury	Grocer
Parade 8 shops	Boots	Chemist
Parade 8 shops	W Aldridge	Ironmonger
Parade 8 shops	Meyer Bros	Fruiterer
Parade 8 shops	F Bentley	Furniture
Parade 8 shops		
Parade 8 shops	H Lewis	Estate Agent
Church Hall		
All Saints Church		
Houses		
Shop	L. Beattie	Photographer
Shop	Wright & Mills	Opticians
Houses		
Baptist Church		
Furzehill Road		
Shop	A Hubbard	Cycle Shop
Shop	Kilby's	Grocer
Shop	F. Cherry	Cobbler
House		
Shop	Byers	Sweets
House		
Shop	S. Hunts	Butcher
House	Dolls' Hospital	Vacant Land
Drayton Road		
Shop	H Bell	Butcher
Shop	Chessell	Wools, Baby Wear,
Shop	W.V.S.	Voluntary work
Shop	Wilkins	Shoe Shop
Houses		
Building	National Provincial Bank	Bank
Station Parade – Shop	H. Alliston	Radio Shop
Station Parade – Shop	Mrs. A.M Kidwell	Post Office, Newsagent
Station Parade – Shop	Groom	Men's Outfitters
Station Parade – Shop	Off Licence	Off Licence
Station Parade – Shop	R. Macnaughton	Chemist
Building	Westminster Bank	Bank

SHENLEY ROAD SHOPS 1920 -1940		
GUIDE SHEETS FOR EARLIER SHOPS AND THEIR LOCATIONS		
NORTH SIDE		
Location	Name of Shop	Retail or Trade
	The Crown Public House	
Building	Barclays Bank	Bank
Shop	E King	Fish
Shop	H. Hastwell	Ironmonger
Shop	C. Pressey	Draper
Glenhaven Avenue		
Shop	EJ Freestone	Baker
Shop	Theobald Farm Dairies	Dairy Products
Shop	Pentecost/S.H. Payne	Florist & Greengrocer
Building	Post Office	Post
House	Poplars	
Wall / Entrance	Dufay Works Entrance	Industrial
Shop	Tom Wingate General Store	General Store
Shop	MacNaughton	Chemist
Shop	Spot Café	
Shop	Radlett Stores	Grocer
Shop	Joanne	Ladies' Hairdresser
Shop	Radlett Stores	Grocer
Building	North Met Electricity	Showroom
Shop	A. Clinton	Barber
Shop	E. Tucker	Drapers
Shop	Roberts / Gilliam	Greengrocer
Shop	Starkes/Hanson's	Confectionery
Building	Central Garage	Garage
Houses	A row of terraced houses	
Clarendon Road		
Shop	Elm Farm Dairies	Dairy
Vacant Land		
3 Shops	Williams	
Vacant Land		
Shop	The Dutch Oven (Freestone)	Bakery
Grosvenor Road		
Vacant Ground	Freestone's Chickens	
Shop		
Shop	Radio Partners	Wireless Sale etc
Shop	Sid's Café	Café
Shop	Wm Haworth	Newsagent

Note. The tables on this page list the buildings that were on either side of Shenley Road in 1940. Most of them were built in the period 1920-1940

C & Q SELF SERVICE STORE
OPENING TODAY
THURSDAY 20TH FEB

CUT PRICES (left) **CUT PRICES** (right)

THE MODERN SELF SERVICE

FREE SUGAR (left) **FREE SUGAR** (right)

GROCER

35 SHENLEY ROAD BOREHAM WOOD

(A FEW DOORS FROM THE MAIN POST OFFICE)

THE LARGEST, RANGE OF OF CUT PRICES IN BOREHAM WOOD

ALL THE LINES AND HUNDREDS MORE SOLD REGULARY AT

CUT PRICES. YOU PAY LESS MORE AT YOUR C & Q

KEILLERS DUNDEE MARMALADE 1/7 1/2
McDOUGALLS SELF RAISING FLOOR 1/9 1/2
ST.MARTINS STRAWBERRY JAM 1/11 1/2
CROSS & BLACKWELL BEANS 8d, 1/-
CROSS & BLACKWELL SPAGHETTI 8d,1/-
MANSTON SILCONE POLISH 1/6 3/-
HEINZE TOMATTO SOUP 11d, 1/3
SELF RAISING FLOOR 1/9 1/2d(3LB BAG)

PORTION OF CHEESE 1/-
PROCESSED PEAS 7 1/2 (10oz tin)
MAXWELL HOUSE 1/11,3/6,9/11
WALLS STEAK & KINDEY PIES 2/9
NESCAFE 1/11, 3/6, 13/3 (large tin)
REGAL EVAPORATION MILK 1/4
BEANS IN TOMATO 8d (8oz tin
BIRD'S JELLIES 9 1/2d.
HEINZ TOMATO KETCHUP 2/1
FRUIT SQUASHES 3/3 BOTTLE
ST.MARTINS LEMON CURD 1/9
ENGLISH GREEN PEAS 1/9
PURE WHITE PEPPER 7d
LUNCHEON MEAT 1/- (7oz tin)
HEINZ BEANS 8d, 1/-
SUGAR 1/1 1/2 2LB
APRICOTES 2/9

HEINZE SPAGHETTI 8d,1/-
BISTO 4/1/2, 8d, 1/3, 2/3
KIT-E-KAT CAT FOOD 9d
KRAFT DAIRYLEA 1/8
RICE MILK PUDDING 1/3
SAXA SALT 5d, 10 1/2d
BRANSTON PICKLE 1/10
OK HP SOURCE 1/6
GOLDEN SHRED SIRUP 1/6
BUTTER 2/4 PER LB
ORANGE MARMALADE 1/4
BIRDS CUSTARD 1/6
PAN-YAN PICKLE 1/10
STEWED STEAK 1/11
CHEF KETCHUP 1/3
LARD 1/4 PER LB
TEA 4d

CHERRY BLOSSOM SHOE POLISH 9d
COLGATE TOOTHPASTE 2/8
GLEEM TOOTHPASTE 2/8
S.R.TOOTHPASTE 2/8

SAVE TIME BLEACH 1/2
FAIRY SNOW, RINSO, 1/4
TIDE.OMO.DAZ 1/6
SANILAY 1/7

Fig 100. [V.R.] 1956 ADVERTISEMENT FOR C &Q SELF SERVICE STORE

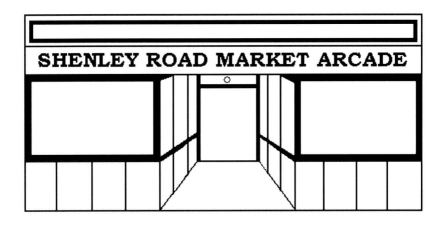

SHENLEY ROAD MARKET ARCADE

THE BISCUIT BOX CUT PRICE GROCERIES	R.J.COLE FRUITERERS
SHOE BOX HAND MADE SHOES	DANNY'S CURTAINS & FURNISHING
MINETTES FASHION WEAR	ALICE BLUE CHILDREN'S BOX PARTY FROCKS,HATS,COATS

T.T.A. DIY SPECIALIST

THE DRESS SHOP	THE HAT BOX MILLINERY,HANDBAGS,BELTS
MILLER'S CHINA SHOP CHINA & TEA SETS	R.COLE & SON CONFECTIONER,CIGS,CHOCS,ICE
SPEN FREE LTD WATCHES, JEWELLERY, REPAIRS	SPENSER WOOLS KNITTING WOOLS

SHENLEY ROAD MARKET ARCADE
OPEN FROM: 9.AM - 6.PM MONDAY TO FRIDAY
TELEPHONE: ELS 1500   (NEXT TO POST OFFICE) TELEPHONE: ELS 1500

Fig 101. [V.R.] 1958 ADVERTISEMENT FOR THE SHENLEY ARCADE

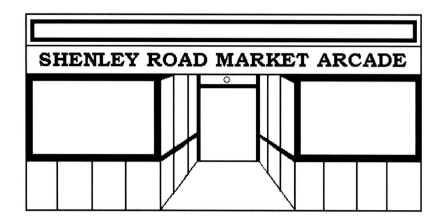

SHENLEY ROAD MARKET ARCADE

DANNY'S BARGAIN BUMPER SALE
FRIDAY JANUARY 27th

CURTAINS NETS 36" WIDE FROM 1/6 PER YARD

FRILLED NETS 36" WIDE FROM 2/3 PER YARD

FURNISHING TAFFETAS 46" WIDE ALL SHADES FROM 2/8 PER YARD

CRETONNES 36" WIDE FROM 2/- PER YARD
CRETONNES 48" WIDE FROM 2/6 PER YARD

BROCADES GOOD QUALITY 36" WIDE FROM 3/11 PER YARD

BROCADES GOOD QUALITY 48" WIDE FROM 4/11 PER YARD

DOUBLE SIZE SHEETS 80" X 100" 29/6 PER PAIR

SINGLE SIZE CANDLEWICK BED SPREADS 72" X 92" 35/-

DOUBLE SIZE CANDLEWICK BED SPREADS 90" X 100" 42/-

A FEW CLEARING LINES BELOW COST PRICES

DORMY 60" X 80" 31/6 & 86" X 100" 55/6

CHEAP WHITNEY BLANKETS

TOWELS 24" X 44" AT 5/- AND 6/6 PER PAIR

BATH TOWELS FULL SIZE 7/11 EACH

SHENLEY ROAD MARKET ARCADE
OPEN FROM: 9.AM - 6.PM MONDAY TO FRIDAY
TELEPHONE: ELS 1500   (NEXT TO POST OFFICE) TELEPHONE: ELS 1502

Fig 102. [V.R.] 1958 ADVERTISEMENT FOR DANNY'S BARGAIN BUMPER SALE

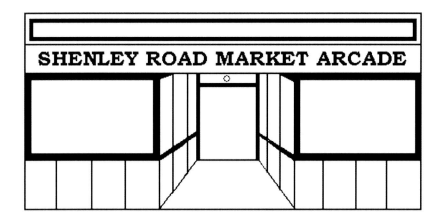

SHENLEY ROAD MARKET ARCADE

MILLERS CHINA & HARDWARE SHOP

SET OF 4 SAUCEPANS   16/11 (WITH LIDS)

HEATMASTER SETS   18/11

EGG TIMERS   18/11

BROOMS   2/6,7/6

KETTLES   6/- & 3/-

CONTEMPORARY TEA SETS 23/6

KITCHEN TEA SETS   16/11

CONVEX MIRRORS   37/6

ORNAMENTS 2/-, 2/6, 2/11

BRONZE PLAQUES   10/-, & 14/-

WALL MIRRORS   ALL 5/-

BASINS, TEA STRAINERS, SCOURERS, SINK PLUNGERS, TOILET BRUSHES

SHENLEY ROAD MARKET ARCADE
OPEN FROM: 9.AM - 6.PM MONDAY TO FRIDAY
TELEPHONE: ELS 1502   (NEXT TO POST OFFICE) TELEPHONE: ELS 1502

Fig 103. [V.R.] 1958 ADVERTISEMENT MILLERS CHINA & HARDWARE SHOP

Fig 104. [V.R.] TYPICAL 1950s PRODUCTS

VIC GOES TO SCHOOL

HIGH CANONS

It must have been around about 1953, while we were waiting for new schools to be built, when I was selected to attend a temporary school called High Canons. It was a very large white mansion situated in Well End, about three miles outside Borehamwood.

The front entrance of High Canons School.

2008

Fig 105. [V.M.]

We travelled there by coach, which picked us up every morning, just across the road from where we lived in Knebworth Path. Every morning, I would cross the road in Nicoll Way, and then board the coach that was waiting to take us to High Canons.

In 1953 we were experiencing some very cold winters with plenty of snow and this always had a picturesque effect on the surrounding countryside.

I had a little school satchel that was packed either with jam or luncheon meat sandwiches made for me by my mother. In those days we could not afford to have school dinners regularly although I did sometimes, but only if my parents had enough money to pay for them!

Before we move on, I have to mention two very sad incidents that happened on February 27th 1953. While we were waiting to board the coach, we were told there had been two fatal accidents. The first accident happened at 8.20 am near Bullens Furnisher Depository in the Elstree Way, which involved a work's bus belonging to the building contractors Gee Walker & Slater. We were told that it had crashed head on into a school coach that was carrying children to High Canons. It was only the skill of the coach driver that prevented the coach from leaving the road with the young passengers and turning the incident into a serious tragedy.

The second incident happened fifteen minutes later at 8.35 am and involved one of our neighbours' children. Their son who was only aged five, sadly died. He was run down by a van that was travelling at high speed down Nicoll Way, about fifty yards away from his home, number 26, Nicoll Way on the L.C.C. Housing Estate. He had toddled over the threshold of his home, and walked along the pavement to join a party of children guarded by adults. The party was being taken by coach to St. Catherine's Elementary School in Barnet where he had started attending just a few weeks before.

The journey to High Canons took about fifteen minutes, and in fact the actual route to this day hasn't changed one bit. The landscape still looks the same as it did fifty-five years ago!

We eventually arrived at the main entrance of High Canons, where we had to drive through some very large wrought-iron gates behind which stood the gatekeeper's house.

The main entrance of High Canons 2005.

Fig 106. [V.R.]

The coach continued along a very long and winding road. Looking through the window, the snow-covered surrounding countryside looked absolutely beautiful. We finally stopped and pulled up outside this very large white building. We were asked to step out and stand in rows on the crispy white snow (no salt in those days!)

We had to wait until we had our name called out by the teacher. Once the names had been checked against the register we followed the teacher into the main entrance hall, where we were given a conducted tour of our school.

I can remember queuing up for our daily entitlement to a quarter of a-pint-of-milk. When it was cold it used to make my nose and head ache when I drank it!

Milk was delivered to the schools by milkmen in steel-wire crates that contained 30 miniature bottles, about six inches high, of wholesome milk. The number of bottles in the crate was about right for a class of children. Straws were provided. Children took turns to be milk monitors.

High Canons, during the spring and summer, was also very picturesque. I remember looking out of the tall windows where I could see beautifully kept gardens that were surrounded by all kinds of shrubs and tall pine trees.In October 2008, I had the opportunity to re-visit my old school. An old friend of mine, who rents a cottage right next to the mansion, asked me if I would like to come and have a look around. I just couldn't resist taking up this opportunity to travel back-in-time; the picture of High Canons, Fig 105, was taken in October 2008. It looks exactly as it did in 1953!

SAFFRON GREEN PRIMARY

The third school I attended was Saffron Green Primary School in Nicoll Way, which opened its doors on the 3rd May 1954. The roll number for the first week was 390, 161 of these being infants who were moved from temporary schools in the area; but mostly from High Canons.

According to the Saffron Green School archives and admission book, I was admitted in that year as pupil number 208 and my last day of attendance was on the 26th July 1957.

We lived directly opposite the school which was very convenient as I could go home for lunch and not have to take sandwiches as I did when I attended High Canons.

Main Entrance of
Saffron Green
Primary School

2003

Fig 107. [V.R.]

On the same site as the school there was a National Health clinic and day nursery which was very handy for my mother who made full use of the facilities while bringing up her young infants and growing children.

The headmaster was Mr. Goodban and our form teacher was Mr. Jones who came from Wales. I can clearly remember that on one occasion, he gave me the slipper right across my backside!

In those days it was a type of punishment that we could receive from a member of staff for being disobedient. The alternative punishment was the cane, which was administered across the palm of our hand!

A typical day at Saffron Green would start around 9 a.m. in the morning and end about 3 p.m. The children, a mixture of boys and girls, would gather in the playground. They were allowed to play outside until it was time to go in for the lessons.

The teacher on duty would then blow a whistle which was a signal to tell the children to stop playing and queue up in rows arranged by form or class teacher.

The children were told to march in single file to their class room where they sat at their desks and waited for the teacher to call out their names to check the register, to see who was present or absent. Once the register had been checked, all the children went to the main hall to attend assembly.

The Main Hall
Saffron Green Primary School
2003

Fig 108. [V.R.]

Practically the whole school, including the teachers, had to attend the morning service, which consisted of prayers and hymns. It was quite common to see and hear one of the teachers playing the piano. After assembly each form would walk back to their classroom, where lessons commenced.

Fig 109. Saffron Green Primary School Badge

HILLSIDE SECONDARY MODERN

The first day of attendance at my last school, Hillside Secondary Modern, was the 9th September 1957. Due to overcrowding, we were assigned to use a temporary church hall in Manor Way.

Manor Hall, Manor Way
Built in 1953
the hall
was used as a
temporary school

2003

Fig 110. [V.R.]

Teachers were allocated to conduct the normal lessons. I can remember on some occasions we had to walk to the main building in Hillside Avenue for certain lessons.

The front entrance of
Hillside School

c1950s

Fig 111. [D.A.]

At Hillside School pupils were expected to wear school uniform. My parents didn't have much money so my mother paid for it with a Provident Cheque, which was one way of borrowing money and then paying it back in weekly instalments.

I had to wear a navy school blazer, which had the school's crest and coat of arms sewn on the top pocket, long grey trousers, white shirt and school tie.

Forth To Adventure

Hillside School Badge

Fig 112. [E.B.W.M.]

Hillside School was much bigger than any of my previous schools. It had a very large hall, stage and balcony. There were some long corridors that led to various class rooms, some of which were laboratories. The school had a gymnasium and sported a very large sports field that had a perimeter probably a couple of miles long. I should know, I used to run around it!

My very first day of attendance at Hillside School was quite a busy one. As they arrived, the new starters had to gather in the main hall where they had to be registered and then placed in different classes, usually known as *forms*. e.g. 1A, 2B, 3C, etc.

The headmaster at the time was Mr. Gernat and Miss Blythe was the headmistress; both had served the school since 1939. Mr. Gernat retired in March 1961.

Our form teacher was Mr. Kuzin who was Polish and was of short build, a little bit podgy, bald and wore round-wire rimmed spectacles; and he also had a cute little turned up nose!

There were teachers for each subject.

Mr. Kuzin,	Maths
Mr. Monswood	History
Mr. Angood	Geography
Miss Durber	Music
Miss Ramsdon	Art
Mr. Sax	P.E.
Mr. O'Keefe	Science
Mr. Hardman	Metalwork
Mr. Hardwood	Woodwork
Mr. Smith	Gardening.

Fig 113. [V.R.] Vic in Hillside Uniform, 1950s

We all had wooden desks, probably dating back to the 1930s or 40s. They had a hinged, lifting top with ink wells that sat in a hole at the front of the desk. The chairs were hard and very uncomfortable.

Mr. Kuzin had one rather memorable habit. During the lessons he would walk around the class room, looking down at what everyone was writing. All of a sudden he would stop and stand over a student and then knock him on the head with his bare knuckles saying *Silly Donkey*! That wouldn't be allowed now!

During some of his lessons, providing we had all been good, he would read us a story instead of the maths lesson. I always looked forward to this moment, especially when he read us a story about *Coco the Clown* who was Russian and became a member of the famous *Bertram Mills Circus.* In later years I was lucky to be able to get hold of a copy of his book that was actually signed by him called *Nicolai Poliakoff - Coco the Clown!*

On our very first lesson we had to draw a time table which consisted of some horizontal and vertical lines finishing up as boxes which had to be filled in with the lessons we would be attending for each day of the week:

Monday	P.E. (Physical Education)	Maths	Geography	History
Tuesday	Maths	Science	Woodwork	Religious Instruction
Wednesday	Gardening	Geography	Metalwork	Music
Thursday	Maths (again!)	History	Science	Art
Friday	P.E.	English.	Religious Instruction	Art

I remember there being different house names, which were Elgar House, Burghley House, Lister House and Salisbury House. The house names were often used and referred to in sports events.

My favourite lessons were Music, Art, English and History. My most disliked lessons, I would say without any hesitation, were Maths and P.E.

There were some funny times during my attendance at Hillside School. On one occasion during an art lessons, when we were all sitting around tables in groups using some powdered paints that we had to mix with water, I, for some unknown reason, decided to blow in the direction of the paint tray and consequently all the different coloured paints were scattered over everyone's faces! This unexpected action caused everyone some great pain of laughter, but it did not impress Miss Ramsdon who immediately summoned me to stand in the front of the class where she gave me a good telling off!

She then told me to go and stand outside the headmaster's office and wait for her. Once inside, Mr. Gernat administered the painful cane across the palm of my hand!

The second time Miss Ramsdon told me off was when she caught me hiding in the art room with a girl during my lunch break. Miss Ramsdon just happened to return at a rather inconvenient time!

In the very last year of my schooling at Hillside the lessons seemed somewhat more relaxed than usual. We went on various outings to museums and visits to the zoo, even Southend-on-Sea!

I remember one occasion when we went with Miss Ramsdon to Aldenham Reservoir. While walking through the woods we came across a film unit who were associated with the Danziger Brothers' film studios. Their studios were situated just beside the reservoir.

The film unit were in the middle of making a film for an ITV television series called *Richard the Lion Heart*. The production for the series started in April 1961 and finished in December 1961. The shooting for each episode took about a week to produce and was reputedly one of their most expensive series ever shown.

Miss Ramsdon asked the director if we could watch them filming. He said that it would be OK providing we kept very quiet so as not to distract the actors during the filming.

The whole experience was very exciting. There were lots of people involved with making the film including actors dressed in medieval armour, directors, cameramen, lighting and sound engineers, make up artists, scenery and prop men and not forgetting the wonderful catering staff!

An old school chum of mine, Michael Cleasby, recently told me that Miss Ramsdon was one of his favourite teachers and reminded me that on one of our art lessons we were invited to visit her home, a little cottage called *The Dell* in Aldeham Village.

One lovely summer's day our class cycled there to see her and when we arrived she greeted us with some food and a glass of fresh orange squash. We all took an immediate interest in her beautiful little old cottage garden where we sat and had our break.

My last year at Hillside School in 1961 seemed to go very quickly. The teachers had made arrangements for a final end of term school dance to be held in the main hall on the last day of our attendance.

We were told that because of this special occasion we could wear whatever we wanted; our school uniforms were now just history! After this exciting news, my mother immediately requested another Provident Cheque so that I could buy some new clothes.

After receiving the cheque, I was allowed to go on my own to buy my clothes, so I went to Girling's, who were a local men's and ladies' outfitters in Shenley Road. Fortunately this shop accepted Provident Cheques which was a way of paying for goods.

I bet that you're all dying to know what clothes I bought. Well! It was the 1960s and you just had to get with it; a green mohair jumper, a white frilly shirt, a black bootlace tie, a pair of very tight black drainpipe trousers, a pair of white socks and finally a pair of brown, extended crocodile-skin *winkle-picker* shoes GO, MAN, GO!

In July 2009 I had the pleasure of revisiting The Dell. When I got there I knocked on the cottage door to ask the owners if they had heard of a Miss Ramsdon ever living there. They advised me that they had never heard of such a person and that the cottage had since those days been made into one house and that they were the present owners. I then asked if I was allowed to take some photographs of the building and the surrounding grounds. I found the only thing that had changed was the original entrance had been blocked off and the cottage was now one complete building instead of a row of cottages, as I remembered it in 1960.

The front of
'The Dell' cottage

2009

Fig 114. [V.R.]

The rear of
'The Dell' cottage

2009

Fig 115. [V.R.]

GOING TO WORK

In 1959, when I was thirteen, I started my very first job working for the *Co-operative Dairies* who were based in Theobald Street.

I had to get up very early on a Saturday morning, get on my bike and cycle down to the Dairy Depot to meet *Alf the milkman*.

Alf was a very nice man who was probably in his late twenties. He had taken over the round from *Tom* who had retired from the job after many years delivering milk to customers in Boreham Wood.

When I arrived, the first thing I had to do was load up the electric milk float with the crates of many varieties of milk that had different coloured tops.

Alf's 1959 Morrison Electric Milk Float

Fig 116. [V.R.]

On board we had silver (semi-skimmed), red (full-cream), blue (half-cream), metal tops (sterilised) and fresh orange. Sometimes the milkman would also carry or sell other items such as eggs, bacon, bread, and butter. Around Christmas time people could even order a *Christmas hamper*!

The Co-operative was not the only supplier of milk in Boreham Wood. There was the *A1 Dairies, later the Express,* who started their operation in Theobald Street in May 1956. Although they had many customers the Co-op were, I think, the first to deliver milk direct to the door step.

After loading the float we set off to commence our round which always started with the industrial estates along the A1 Barnet By-Pass. The first factory was Opperman's, followed by the The Royal National Life Boat Institution (R.N.L.I.). We always drove straight into their yard. There were three cottages on the site that were occupied by some of the employees.

Having delivered to all the factories we started delivering to the housing estates.

Starting with Ripon Way Alf would tell me what milk I had to deliver to the different houses. I would then take the appropriate colour top from the milk crates and carry the bottles in my hands, usually with the necks between the knuckles of my fingers.

The milk bottles were then placed onto the customer's doorstep. Sometimes we collected empty bottles that were usually cleaned by the customer. Some not!

There were days when the customer would invite us into their home for a cup of tea. I can remember one occasion when Alf got invited in for a cuppa at a customer's house in Dacre Gardens, but this time I had to stay outside and sit in the van and wait for him. It was a very cold day and just before he went in, I asked him if he could ask the customer if I could use the toilet. He said he would ask, but it seemed a very long time before he came back out; by then it was too late!

Eventually, Alf came out, and he said that he had completely forgotten about asking for me. He looked down at the front of my trousers where he could clearly see that I had had a slight accident; pointing his finger, he just stood there and laughed his head off! At which point, he apologised and said that he thought that it would be better if he took me home to change my trousers. He had to explain to my mother what had happened. We then continued with the rest of the round.

Although my next after-school job was actually in 1960, I feel I have to tell you the story of my time working for two of our local shops in Howard Drive.

In those days the shops were very small and nothing like the big supermarkets of today. All the customers were very happy with what they had. It was very convenient and the people who worked in these shops were always polite and friendly.

The first one was *Tilson's*, our greengrocer, who I worked for in the early part of the year, after school hours and all day on Saturdays. My duties included looking after all the fruit and vegetables, making sure the shelves were kept full and keeping the shop clean and tidy. Sometimes on a Saturday morning I had to boil the beetroot!

The second shop where I worked, which was next door, was *Taylor Brothers*, a grocer. I started there sometime in the middle of the year. I worked in this shop everyday after school and all day on Saturdays. My job was to keep all the shelves stocked up with the groceries.

There were counters running down both sides of the shop. On one side we had all our cold meats like ham, corned beef, spam, liver sausages and bacon. The counter on the other side held eggs, tea, coffee, sugar, jam, marmalade, cereals, biscuits, cakes, soap powders and many other products that were usually associated with this type of shop.

Mr. Pollard, the shop manager, would always be standing at the far end of the counter where he personally undertook the responsibility of slicing the cold meats. This was probably because of Health & Safety as he used a slicing machine which had a very sharp and round blade about 6 inches diameter. There was a small handle, which when turned, rotated the blade to cut the different types of meats. It could be set to cut whatever thickness the customer wanted.

One of my other responsibilities was to deliver groceries to the customers. I had a bike that had a carrying cradle fitted at the front, just below the handle bars. This was used to carry the box that had been filled with groceries by the shop assistant.

The Taylor Brothers Delivery Bike 1960

Fig 117. [V.R.]

This is how it worked. A customer would visit the shop and give a list of their groceries to one of the shop assistants who would then pick all the items from the shelves and place them in a suitably sized cardboard box. As soon as the groceries had been picked, I had to deliver them to the customer's home on one of the local housing estates.

When I arrived at the address I had to lift the box from the cradle and carry it to the customer's front door where I had to either knock or ring the bell. The customer then opened the door and took their groceries. Sometimes, if I was lucky, I would get a tip!

I can remember that on one occasion, as I was delivering groceries to one of the customers I stood my bike against the kerb stone and as I walked away to check the house number my bike suddenly fell over and all the groceries came out of the box and spread onto the pavement!

Arriving back at the shop Mr. Pollard, the manager, was waiting for me and judging by the look on his face, he didn't look very happy. He then told me that he had had a phone call and complaint from one of the customers about receiving damaged groceries! With this bad news, Mr. Pollard said that I would have to pay for them out of my wages!

Another incident at the shop was when Mr. Pollard showed me how to peel the wax from the cheese barrels. With the aid of a very sharp knife, he would cut into the wax, then lifting and gradually peeling it back, the same way you would peel a banana, he then continued until he had completely removed all the wax and outer protection from the barrel.

The next stage was to cut the cheese into segments. He did this by using a tool that was just basically a length of steel wire with a wooden handle at each end, which he would hold in each hand, then place the wire on the top and centre of the barrel, push downwards and repeat the procedure, cutting across the other section of the barrel. This was similar to cutting a birthday cake! He ended up with four matching segments.

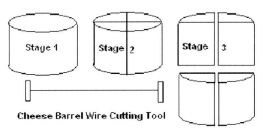

Slicing a cheese

Fig 118. [V.R.]

After my demonstration, Mr Pollard said that he had to get back to serving the customers and that I would have to get on with doing the next barrel on my own.

I started by cutting into the wax but I found that I had some difficulty with peeling the wax like Mr. Pollard had shown me. All I seemed to be doing was continuously stabbing the surface with the knife, creating a load of holes and craters, making it look just like the moon!

It was now time for me to come clean and tell Mr. Pollard exactly what I had done, so I went to the front of the shop where he was in the middle of serving a customer. I then politely asked him if he could spare me a minute and when he came around the back his face looked as if he'd just seen a ghost!

There was definitely something about the way we used to do our shopping, all the shops were smaller and, compared with nowadays, the people who worked in them had a polite and friendly manner when serving customers.

After leaving school in July 1961 I was very lucky because my father was able to get me a job working for **Elliott Brothers (London) Ltd.,** the same firm that he worked for. I started there in September 1961 as a general office and administration clerk.

Pounds, shillings and pence: £.s.d. or £/s/d

Our money was in £.s.d. until 1971 when Britain converted to decimal currency.
The *d* stood for denarius, a Roman coin.
Various coins and notes could be used to make a pound, £1.

Coin	Also known as	Number to the £	Number to the shilling
Shilling	bob	20	
Florin		10	
Crown		4	
Half-crown		8	
10 shilling note	10 bob note	2	
Penny		240	12
Sixpence	tanner	40	2
Halfpenny	pronounced hayp'ny	480	24
Farthing		960	48
Three penny piece	thruppenny bit	80	
One pound note	quid	1	

For *ten bob (50p)* we could buy sixteen pounds of sugar. A bar of chocolate cost a *tanner.* Betting and expensive goods were in guineas, which were worth 21 shillings each, but there was no guinea coin. Happy days! We understood it but foreigners thought it quaint.

Finances

WHAT PEOPLE WERE EARNING IN APRIL 1950

Presented in old money Pounds, Shillings and pence, £.s.d.

The figures for average weekly earnings are calculated for the last pay-week in April 1950. The Pay-rates and earnings are for men over 21 and women of 18 and over.

INDUSTRY

Minimum Weekly Wage	£.	s.	d.		£.	s.	d.
Agricultural Labourers	5.	0.	0.				
Bank Clerks	3.	13.	1.	"	4.	6.	7.
Bricklayers	6.	1.	0.	"	6.	12.	0.
Bus and Tram Conductors	4.	17.	6.	"	6.	5.	0.
Coal Miners Underground	6.	0.	0.	"	9.	3.	6.
Coal Miners Surface	5.	5.	0.	"	6.	11.	10
Cotton Weavers Men	3.	14.	2.				
Cotton Weavers Women	3.	14.	2.				
Dockers	5.	4.	6.	"	7.	16.	4.
Electricity Workers	5.	5.	5.	"	6.	0.	1
Fitters	5	7.	0.				
Gas Workers	4.	19.	0.	"	5.	11.	10
Iron and Steel Workers	5.	1.	9.				
Metropolitan Policemen	6.	10.	10				
Qualified Teachers Men	5.	15.	5.				
Qualified Teachers	5.	3.	10.				
Railway Porters Grade 2	4.	16.	0.	"	4.	19.	0.
Shop Assistants (Cooperative) Men	5.	6.	6.	"	5.	17.	0.
Shop Assistants (Cooperative) Women	4.	1.	0.	"	4.	7.	6.
Shorthand Typists (Civil Servants)	3.	16.	0.				
Soldiers and Airmen Private and A.C.2.	2.	9.	0.				
Soldiers and Airman Sergeant	5.	15.	6.				
Soldiers and Airman 2nd Lt. & Pilot Officer	6.	2.	6.				
Staff Nurses	6.	1.	2				

A Taste of Shopping in the 1950s

1950s Prices:		
Product	**Cost in £.s.d.**	**Cost in Decimal**
Medium Horlicks	3s 4d	18p
Small salad cream	1s 1d	6p
Small Fray Bentos pie	2s 3d	12p
6 Oxo Cubes	9d	4p
12 standard eggs	4s 3d	21p
1b Magic Stork margarine	1s 1d	6p
1b Lyons Tips tea	1s 4p	7p
2lb granulated sugar	1s 3d	7p
1 Delsey toilet roll	1s 3d	7p
1b streaky bacon	1s 5d	8p
2oz jar Marmite	1s 6d	8p
Small Heinz ketchup	1s 4d	7p
Medium Omo	1s 9d	9p
Cross & Blackwell beans	8d	3p
1lb New Zealand butter	2s 2d	11p

Nostalgia!   -   Listening to the Radio

In the 1950s almost everyone owned a radio for home entertainment and news until television became affordable and widespread.

The Rowntree Family *Bush Radio*

1954

Fig 119. [V.R.]

I have fond memories of listening to the radio which was usually switched on most of the time. There were so many different programmes to listen to that were always very entertaining, programmes like the following.

The Archers
Billy Cotton Band Show
Educating Archie
Two Way Family Favourites
Friday Night is Music Night
The Goon Show
Have a Go
In Town Tonight
Journey into Space
Life with the Lyons
Listen with Mother
Mrs. Dale's Diary
Much Binding in the Marsh
Music While You Work
The Navy Lark
Take it from Here
Woman's Hour
Workers' Playtime.
Paul Temple

My mother and father had their own favourites to listen to. Sometimes, such as on a Sunday at 12 noon when *Two Way Family Favourites* was broadcast, we all listened to the same programme. This was a popular record request programme designed to link families at home in the UK with *British Forces Posted Overseas* (BFPO).

The forerunner was aired during World War II on the General Forces programme. Titled *Forces Favourites*. Their families at home could request a favourite record along with a dedication. At the end of the war, the show was renamed *Two Way Family Favourites* and broadcast on the BBC Light Programme. The two regular presenters were *Jean Metcalfe* and *Cliff Michelmore*. It ran from 1945 until 1984.

There were times when the home atmosphere got a bit tense, especially when the news or the sports programmes came on, when my father wanted to check the pools results. We never had any luck with it! In later years when we had a television set the same rule applied "*Keep quiet!*"

As I grew older listening to music on the radio was one of my favourite pastimes. I probably got more interested towards the end of the 1950s when *Rock-'n'-Roll* started to hit the music scene in a big way.

I have put together some of my own 1950s favourites, which you might remember.

1950-52
She Wears Red Feathers	Guy Mitchell
The Drinking Song, Because You're Mine	Mario Lanza
Auf Wiedersehen	Vera Lynn

1953
Wonderful Copenhagen	Danny Kaye
Oh Mein Papa, Zambesi	Eddie Calvert
I Saw Mummy Kissing Santa Claus	The Beverley Sisters
Poppa Piccolino	Ray & Diana Decker
That's Amore	Dean Martin

1954
Softly Softly	Ruby Murray
Gilly Gilly Ossenpfeffer Katzenellenbogen by the Sea	Max Bygraves
Mambo Italiano	Rosemary Clooney
Secret Love, Black Hills of Dakota	Doris Day
Happy Wanderer	Obernkirchen Children's Choir

1955
Mr Sandman	Max Bygraves
Stranger in Paradise	Alma Cogan
Dreamboat, Smile	Nat King Cole
Rock Around the Clock	Bill Haley and the Comets
Hernando's Hideaway	Johnson Brothers
The Man from Larami	Al Martino
The Yellow Rose of Texas, Robin Hood	Gary Miller

1956
The Ballard Of Davy Crocket	Max Bygraves
Why Do Fools Fall in Love	Frankie Lymon and The Teenagers
Memories Are Made of This	Dean Martin

1957
Love Letters in the Sand, April Love, Speedy Gonzales	Pat Boone
Diana	Paul Anker
When I Fall in Love	Nat King Cole
Cumberland Gap, Putting On the Style	Lonnie Donegan
Save the Last Dance for Me	The Drifters
Bye Bye Love, Wake Up Little Susie	The Everly Brothers
Great Balls of Fire	Jerry Lee Lewis
Long Tall Sally	Little Richard
Peggy Sue	Buddy Holly

How Much Is That Doggie in the Window	Patti Page
1958	
You Need Hands, Tulips from Amsterdam	Max Bygraves
Chantilly Lace	The Big Bopper
Kiss Me, Honey Honey, Kiss Me	Shirley Bassey
Tequila	The Champs
Lollipop	The Chordettes
Lollipop	The Mudlarks
Summertime Blues, C'mon Everybody	Eddie Cochran
Magic Moments, Catch a Falling Star	Perry Como
Tom Dooley	Lonnie Donegan
All I Have To Do Is Dream, Bird Dog	The Everly Brothers
Who's Sorry Now, Carolina Moon	Connie Francis
The Story of My Life	Michael Holliday
Rave On	Buddy Holly
Hoots Mon	Lord Rockingham's X1
Volare	Dean Martin
Twilight Time	The Platters
1959	
Jingle Bell Rock	Max Bygraves
Mack the Knife, Hello Dolly	Louis Armstrong
Seven Little Girls Sitting in the Back Seat	The Avons
Sing Little Birdie	Pearl Carr and Teddy Johnson
Ragtime Cowboy Joe	The Chipmunks
Side Saddle	Russ Conway
Dream Lover, Mack the Knife	Bobby Darin
Does Your Chewing Gum Loose Its Flavour, Battle	Lonnie Donegan
Of New Orleans	
What Do You Want	Adam Faith
What Do Want To Make Those Eyes at Me for	Emile Ford
Maybe Tomorrow	Billy Fury
Heart Beat, It Doesn't Matter Anymore, Peggy Sue	Buddy Holly
Red River Rock	Johnny and the Hurricanes
Rawhide	Frankie Laine
It's Late	Ricky Nelson
Mary's Boy Child	Nina and Frederick
Smoke Gets in Your Eyes	The Platters
Living Doll	Cliff Richard

I can clearly remember my parents one Christmas in the 1950s buying me my first radio. It was made by Philips and was a valve radio with a blue plastic outer case. It had three little white square push-down buttons located at the front; these were for selecting the different radio stations.

I can't quite remember where my parents bought it. It may have been *Janes & Adams* shop in Shenley Road, because the other and oldest shop, *Geo. D. Lilley's* was no longer around at that time. I can remember a few weeks just before Christmas looking in the shop window and seeing it on display, and wishing that I might be the lucky one to find it under our Christmas tree!

The night before Christmas, I couldn't sleep nor stop thinking about this radio and when it was time to get up and open our presents, my dreams had come true. Thanks Mum and Dad (& Father Christmas of course!)

Still feeling very excited, I just sat there all day just staring at my radio and looking forward to trying it out. That night I went to bed with the lights turned off. I then turned the radio on and after a short while I could see the valves glowing through the front panel which made it look quite cool! I started twiddling the knobs to find the different radio stations, especially *Radio Luxemburg*, the station which everyone had difficulty tuning into.

Some of my friends weren't so lucky, they had to persevere with their crystal sets, I never ever owned one, but I think I did listen to one at some stage in my youth.

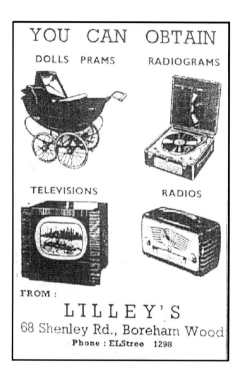

Advertisement for
Geo. D. Lilley's
radio and television services

1952

Fig 120.

Lilley's Shop Window

Fig 121. [E.B.W.M.]

More Nostalgia - Going to the Pictures

In the 1950s, going to the pictures was the *in-thing*, not only did Boreham Wood have its own cinema it also had its own film studios where they made many of the films that were later shown at our local cinema.

When we first arrived in Boreham Wood we were not aware there was a cinema in Shenley Road and it wasn't until about 1953 that we started to attend the performances.

The cinema named the *Studio* was built in 1935 and first opened its doors in 1936.

In 1966 it underwent some alterations and was renamed *Studio 70.* Due to poor attendance the final performance was on the 6th June 1981. Sadly, the cinema was demolished in December 1981.

Front view of the Studio Cinema

built 1935

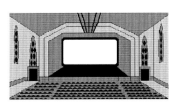

Inside the Studio Cinema 820 seat auditorium

Fig 122. [V.R.]

There were other cinemas near to Boreham Wood, but you had to travel by bus to see the films, in Barnet there were the Gaumont, the Regal and the Odeon, in Watford, the Empire, the Essoldo, the Carlton and the Plaza.

The 1950s was to be one of the greatest decades and one of the most popular times for going to the cinema. My father used to make sure that we went to our local *Studio Cinema* at least once a week. I can clearly remember that he always looked in the Boreham Wood & Elstree Post to see what films were on at our local cinema. If there was nothing interesting showing, he would then look at what was on at the cinemas in the other locations.

The films would, however, eventually finish up being shown in our own local cinema if you didn't want to be bothered with travelling.

There were different viewing times for the performances depending on the types of films being shown. For example, programmes times might have been: 2.00, 2.40, 3.20, 3.30, 4.45, 5.30, 5.50, 6.25, 7.30, 8.15, 8.40, 9.25 p.m.

There were different prices for the seats: 1/6d (7.5p), 2/- (10p), 2/3d (12p), and 3/- (15p). Seats on some performances could be reserved and booked in advance; for this privilege it would cost you 3d (1.5p) and 6d (2.50p) extra.

We always left home about six-thirty in the evening allowing us enough time to catch a 107 or 306 bus outside the Holy Cross Church in Balmoral Drive and get off outside the A.B.P.C. Studios in Shenley Road.

Having crossed the road we popped into a little confectionary shop called **Candies** where my father bought us some sweets or chocolates to take with us; they did sell some sweets in the cinema, but they were always more expensive!

We then headed for the cinema which was only a few yards up the road, just past the Red Lion Pub. Once inside the foyer my father then queued up to buy our tickets. We then proceeded towards the auditorium where we were greeted by the usherette who was holding a torch she used to check our tickets and show us to our seats.

The auditorium had 820 seats of differing prices for the stalls, middle, sides, front and the circle which was located upstairs. We always sat on the sides, because the seats were the cheapest!

Inside, it was dimly lit but there would be some music playing which sounded as if it was coming from behind the huge curtains that were hanging in front of the screen. In the old days there would have been an organist sitting at the front of the stage playing some popular tunes.

I can remember on some occasions it was very dark and the film had already started, so we had to ask other people to stand up to allow us to get to our seat; they weren't always happy about this brief interruption!

As we sat in our seats waiting for the film to start, we saw other people coming in and being shown to their seats and it wasn't long before the auditorium was filled. When everyone was seated, the lights were turned down and the curtains opened exposing the big screen and the film commenced. The show started with advertisements and newsreels that were followed by a cartoon or short feature film.

After the feature film there was usually an intermission when the lights were turned on and the music would start playing again.

Normally an usherette stood in front of the stage selling ice-cream tubs and choc-ices. Sometimes, if the cinema was busy, the lights started to go back down which meant that the main film was about to start. The unlucky ones who hadn't time to buy any ice-cream rushed to find their seats, and sometimes went through the same ritual of asking people to stand up so they could get to their own seats.

There was also a very smoky atmosphere because smoking in those days wasn't banned in public places! After all this palaver the audience could finally settle down and get on with watching what had been paid for, the film!

In the introduction of my book, I mentioned that there used to be a medieval castle standing on a hill next to the M.G.M. Film Studios which was part of a set that was built for the film, *Ivanhoe* starring Robert Taylor and Elizabeth Taylor. This film was made in 1952 and was first shown at the Boreham Wood *Studio Cinema* on Thursday 5th March 1953. It was given a *U* certificate.

The castle stood there for many years but the site is now a modern housing estate. I can remember seeing this castle especially when travelling on the bus to the Village. When we first saw it we thought it was real! Sheep were usually grazing in the fields in front of the castle.

MGM's Castle

Fig 123 [V.R.]

A drawing of the MGM 'castle 1952

In 1957 there were strong rumours that Boreham Woods's famous *cardboard castle* built in 1951 in the grounds of the M.G.M. was to be demolished. The castle had become a familiar landmark and had been featured in several films made by the studio. However, it was decided that the landmark would remain a little bit longer.

At the time an M.G.M. spokesman said there were no plans for doing away with the whole castle. Only one wall erected specially for the film *The Black Knight* was to be pulled down and the appearance of the castle would be preserved.

The castle was originally built for making medieval films, including *Ivanhoe, Quentin Durward, Knights of the Round Table* and *The Black Knight*. The castle continued to interest visitors travelling to Boreham Wood when they saw what they thought was an ancient monument.

We were soon familiar with the surrounding world of film-making, learning to accept that to make the films we had to put up with some inconveniences. In March 1954 residents complained about the noise coming from the A.B.P.C. Studios who were using a jet engine to create waves in a huge water tank for the film *Moby Dick* starring *Gregory Peck*. One housewife said the noise was deafening. But it was something the residents got used to. Another woman said it was difficult to get her children to sleep when the engine started up. Complaints had also come from people who lived half a mile away in Hartforde Road who said that when the wind was blowing in their direction they could hear the engine quite clearly. One resident in Boreham Wood described the noise as a *"right racket!"*

I can clearly remember a similar incident. I think that it may have also been in 1954 when the A.B.P.C film studios were in the process of making *Dam Busters* which was actually released and first shown in the Studio Cinema in September 1955.

It was one night during the week when I had gone to bed early because I had to go to school the very next day. I was lying in bed quite happily sleeping like a log, when suddenly, I was woken up and disturbed by this very loud banging sound which was coming from outside. As I opened my eyes I could see the whole room flashing with this very bright light which at first I thought was lightning! Following this there was a very loud explosion, which again I thought was thunder! If I remember correctly it went on for a very long time and it became quite frightening, so I hid under the bed covers! This activity started and finished very late in the evening, I would say right up to about midnight.

I called out to my mother and father who were still up downstairs having their last 'smoke' before they went to bed. My father shouted up to me and said *"Don't be frightened son. It's only the film studios making a war film"*.

In *July 1952* Boreham Wood opened its first Saturday morning cinema in the adapted Village Hall in Shenley Road showing serial cartoons and adventure stories exclusively for children. There was an estimated audience of 300 children, which filled the hall to capacity.

The Village Hall in
Shenley Road was used as
Boreham Wood's
first Saturday morning
Cinema
in 1952

2008

Fig 124. [V.R.]

It was the idea of Mr. George Lilley who was a local trader and owned a radio and television shop on the corner of Shenley Road and Furzehill Road. He decided to organise and sponsor the cinema out of his own pocket.

The programmes were limited to two two-hour sessions: 9 am to 11 am, 11 am to 1 pm, the price for admission was 9d. (4p). Although limited to a single projector, the cinema featured fresh films from general distribution circuits such as the J. Arthur Rank Children's Club Entertainment.

Eventually, Saturday morning pictures was transferred to the big Studio Cinema and this is when I started to attend; it became a very exciting time for the youngsters of Boreham Wood.

The films were shown in the morning instead late evenings when children normally had to go with their parents. I believe it started around about 9 am and finished at 12 pm.

The films were selected purely for children's entertainment, especially serial films like *Superman, the Lone Ranger and Tonto, Hopalong Cassidy* (I hated his hat!), *Roy Rogers, Zorro, Tarzan, cartoons and newsreels*. One of my all time favourites was *The Little Rascals*.

We would sometimes travel by bus if it was raining, but we usually walked.

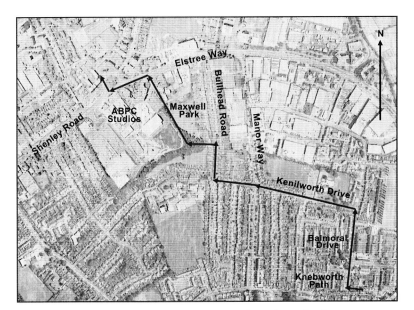

Fig 125.   Our route from Knebworth Path to the Cinema
took us through a large field known as Maxwell Park

Sometimes, after the performance, we would wander down to the Village to look at the shops; probably to spend the rest of our pocket money!

I think that going to the cinema in those days made teenagers very adventurous. Many of us just couldn't wait to get home and play pretend games, trying to copy many of the films that we had seen; especially the cowboy ones!

Sadly, the habit of going to the pictures gradually came to an end because by the end of the 1950s everyone decided that it was time for a change in family entertainment and invest in a television. People felt that it would be better to stay in the comfort of their own homes instead of going out; especially on cold winter nights when they would have to wait and queue at bus stops freezing to death. It was easier to sit in an armchair, turn on a little switch and sit back and enjoy an evening's entertainment on the television. However, at that time television sets only had a 9 or 12 inch screen and were only in black and white, while cinema screens were large and some films were in colour.

Censorship

Film Censors checked films before they were released and ordered bits to be cut out if they thought they might be offensive. When they were happy they gave the film a Certificate, *U* meant the film was suitable for children, *A* meant Adults only, and *X* meant the film might contain nasty scenes.

During the 1920s the release of a locally made film depicting the execution of Edith Cavell (Dawn, 1928, directed by Herbert Wilcox, starring Dame Sybil Thorndike as Nurse Edith Cavell), caused protests from the German Embassy and the British Censor tried to refuse giving a Certificate. After a few small changes the film was shown anyway!

FILMS SHOWN AT THE STUDIO CINEMA 1953-1959

*** Films made in Boreham Wood

Year	Date	Name of Film	Cert	Actors Names
1953	05.03	Ivanhoe***	U	Robert & Elizabeth Taylor
1953	03.09	The Cruel Sea	U	Jack Hawkins
1953	31.12	Peter Pan	U	Walt Disney
1954	22.04	Calamity Jane	U	Doris Day, Howard Keel
1954	03.05	Snow White & The Seven Dwarfs	U	Walt Disney
1954	02.09	Genevieve	U	John Gregson, Dinah Sheridan, Kenneth More.
1954	02.09	His Majesty O' Keefe	U	Burt Lancaster
1954	21.10	The Black Knight ***	U	Alan Lad, Patricia Mendina
1954	04.11	Apache	U	Burt Lancaster, Jean Peters
1954	11.11	Elephant Walk	U	Elizabeth Taylor, Peter Finch
1954	23.12	Alice in Wonderland	U	Walt Disney
1954		Moby Dick ***	U	Gregory Peck
1955	31.03	Three Coins in a Fountain	U	Dorothy McGuire, Jean Peters, Louis Jourdan
1955	09.05	The Student Prince	U	Ann Blyth, Edmund Purdom & The voice of Mario Lanza
1955	07.07	Above us the Waves	U	John Mills, John Gregson, Donald Sinden
1955	04.08	Long John Silver	U	Robert Newton
1955	11.08	White Christmas	U	Bing Crosby, Danny Kaye
1955	12.09	The Dam Busters ***	U	Richard Todd, Michael Redgrave
1955	27.10	Seven Brides for Seven Brothers	U	Jane Powell, Howard Keel
1955	03.11	A Kid for Two Farthings	U	Celia Johnson, Diana Dors, David Kossoff
1955	24.11	The Man from Laramie	U	James Stewart
1955	19.12	Twenty Thousand Leagues Under the Sea	U	Kirk Douglas
1956	22.03	To Catch a Thief	A	Cary Grant, Grace Kelly
1956	05.04	Lady and the Tramp	U	Walt Disney
1956	12.04	The White Feather	U	Robert Wagner, John Lund
1956	10.04	Cockle Shell Heroes	U	Jose Ferror, Trevor Howard
1956	03.05	Davy Crockett	U	Walt Disney
1956	17.05	Helen of Troy	U	
1956	30.08	Genevieve (second showing)	U	Kenneth More, John Gregson
1956	17.09	Reach for the Sky	U	Kenneth More
1956	17.09	The Last Hunt	U	Stewart Granger, Robert Taylor
1956	04.10	Richard III	U	Laurence Olivier, Claire Bloom
1956	01.11	Carousel	U	Gordon Macbae, Shirley Tones
1956	24.12	Trapeze	U	Burt Lancaster, Tony Curtis, Gina Lollobrigida
1956	28.02	The King and I	U	Deborah Kerr, Yul Brynner
1956	18.02	The Battle of the River Plate	U	John Gregson, Peter Finch
1957	18.02	The Red Balloon	U	

1957	28.02	The Last Wagon	A	Richard Widmark
1957	14.03	The Fastest Gun Alive	A	Glen Ford, Jean Crain
1957	04.04	Hollywood or Bust	U	Dean Martin & Jerry Lewis
1957	22.08	Lady and the Tramp	U	Walt Disney (second showing)
1957	21.10	Wyatt Earp	A	Burt Lancaster, Kirk Douglas
1958	13.02	Loving You	U	Elvis Presley, Elizabeth Scott
1958	03.03	The Bridge on the River Kwai	U	William Holden, Alex Guinness, Jack Hawkins
1958	13.03	The Pyjama Game	U	Doris Day
1958	27.03	The Pride and the Passion	U	Cary Grant, Frank Sinatra, Sophia Loren
1958	24.04	A Tale of Two Cities	U	Dirk Bogard, Cecil Parker, Dorothy Tutin
1958	15.05	Jail House Rock	A	Elvis Presley
1958	07.07	Dunkirk		John Mills, Bernard Lee, Richard Attenborough
1958	28.08	Cinderella	U	Walt Disney
1958	01.09	The Vikings	A	Kirk Douglas, Tony Curtis, Janet Leigh
1958	30.10	A Night to Remember	U	Kenneth More
1958	03.11	Ice Cold in Alex***	A	John Mills, Sylvia Syms
1958	04.12	Seven Hills of Rome	U	Mario Lanza
1958	11.12	The Left Handed Gun	A	Paul Newman, Lita Milan
1959	23.02	I was Monty's Double	U	John Mills, Cecil Parker
1959	09.03	The Inn of the Sixth Happiness***	U	Ingrid Bergman, Curt Jurgens, Robert Donat
1959	26.03	The Square Peg	U	Norman Wisdom
1959	06.04	Fantasia	U	Walt Disney
1959	13.04	Operation Amsterdam	U	Peter Finch, Eva Bartok
1959	11.05	Danger Within	U	Richard Todd, Bernard Lee
1959	21.05	The Bridge on the River Kwai	U	Alec Guinness, William Holden, Jack Hawkins (second showing)
1959	20.08	The Big Country	A	Gregory Peck, Jean Simmons, Charlton Heston, Burl Ives
1959	12.10	Serious Charge	X	Anthony Quayle, Ray Churchill
1959	09.11	Jack the Ripper	X	Lee Paterson, Eddie Syrne
1959	17.12	King of the Wild Frontier	U	Walt Disney
1959	21.12	Tom Thumb	U	Russ Tamblyn, Peter Sellers, Terry Thomas
1959	28.12	The Wizard of Oz	U	Judy Garland

Watching Television

My family's first introduction to television was in 1953, the year of the Coronation of Queen Elizabeth II, which took place 2nd June. It was the first coronation to be televised live by the BBC.

This historic event prompted people to buy or rent a television (probably their first!). Many people who couldn't afford one were invited to watch their neighbour's!

I can remember doing exactly that, especially on the day of the Coronation when our next door neighbours had invited us around to their house at 22 Nicoll Way to see the event on their brand new television.

This was what our next door neighbour's television set looked like in 1953

Fig 126. [V.R.]

As we walked into their living room we were asked to remove our shoes and as I looked around I couldn't help but notice their new television standing in the corner looking just like a piece of furniture, only it was slightly different. It had a 12 inch glass screen (the picture tube) that was enclosed in a beautifully finished veneered wooden cabinet. Fitted to this were two doors with some decorative handles that could be closed when no one was watching the television.

After watching this event we went home and it was a rather strange feeling walking into our sitting room realising that there was something missing. Yes, that's right, a television!

I think that at the time, there could possibly have been a bit of jealousy and thinking to ourselves, why haven't we got one? Were we too poor to be able to afford one?

Our neighbours were always very sympathetic and continued allowing us to watch their television until we had our own one. It was during these visits that we learned what programmes were being televised by the BBC.

I have many fond memories of watching their television, here are some of the wonderful programmes that we watched:

Andy Pandy	first televised 11th July 1950
Come Dancing	first televised 29th September 1950
What's My Line	first televised 16th July 1951

Bill and Ben, the Flowerpot Men	first televised 18th December 1952
The Coronation of Queen Elizabeth II	televised 2nd June 1953
The Quatermass Experiment	first televised 18th July 1953
Rag, Tail and Bobtail	first televised 10th September 1953
The Grove Family	first televised 2nd April 1954

The Introduction of TV Licences

Fig 127.

Please Remember
TO BUY YOUR £2 TELEVISION LICENCE AS SOON AS YOUR SET IS INSTALLED. AND CLAIM THE REBATE DUE TO YOU ON YOUR UNEXPIRED £1 LICENCE WHICH IS FOR SOUND ONLY

During the early 1950s it became compulsory for anyone who owned or rented a television set to acquire a television licence; a radio licence on its own was not acceptable for watching television.

In the month of November 1954, it was announced in the Boreham Wood & Elstree Post that the television licence detector vans were visiting the area and anyone caught without a licence would be fined or prosecuted!

This news came as a warning and many people rushed out to buy one. Eight residents who didn't bother went to court and were fined between £1 and £2, at the worst it could have been as much as £20!

Having a TV licence didn't necessarily give one the green-light to be able to watch one's television. At that time in Boreham Wood there were certain rules that were imposed by the L.C.C. (London County Council) who had made it quite clear to their new tenants that, before erecting a television aerial on the roof of their properties, they should apply for permission before going ahead.

In September 1955 the L.C.C. took the view that outdoor aerials presented an unsightly appearance and it was their practice to encourage their tenants to install them internally. If however, the reception proved to be unsatisfactory, the council would consider individual applications for an outdoor aerial.

Eventually we got our first television in 1955 and I must say that it came as a bit of a surprise as my parents had kept it a complete secret. (Our aerial was in the loft!)

It all happened one day when I arrived home from school and went straight into our sitting room and I saw our new television standing in the corner. It was a very exciting time for everyone and we just couldn't wait to watch our favourite programmes on our own television.

The Rowntree Family's first television set

1955

Fig 128. [V.R.]

The arrival of our television couldn't have come at a better time, because in the same year ITV began broadcasting programmes and commercials. One of the very first advertisements was for **Gibbs SR Toothpaste** which was televised in September 1955 (about the time we got our television). Other adverts were for **Capstan Cigarettes, Esso Blue Paraffin, Cadum Soap, Rowntree's Fruit Gums, Rael Brook** (Men's Shirts) **Tide** (Soap Powder) **Strand** (Cigarettes); to name just a few.

At the beginning of commercial television there were literally hundreds of other adverts being shown on the ITV channels. I always enjoyed watching them. However, in time I eventually found that the commercial break became rather annoying, especially when I was in the middle of watching a good western or something else interesting!

We were lucky to have two channels which gave us a choice of what programmes to watch. I could put my hand on my heart and honestly say that we probably watched the ITV channels more than the BBC programmes. The ITV seemed to have more choice and variety. However, at least we were still privileged with being able to watch some of our favourite BBC programmes that we had seen for the first time on our next door neighbour's television in 1953. Most of these were still running, even in 1955.

In 1955 we saw the introduction of two new channels: Rediffusion who began transmitting on the 22nd September 1955, followed by ATV (Associated Television) on 24th September 1955.

Some more television programmes. * denotes date first televised

1955:	
Picture Book	14th February*
Life with the Lyons	29th June*
Dixon of Dock Green	9th July*
This is your Life	29th July*
The Wooden Tops	9th Sept.*
Crackerjack	14th Sept.*
1956	
Winter Olympics	26th Jan.*

Billy Cotton Band Show	22nd May*
Eurovision Song Contest	24th May*
Hancock's Half Hour	6th July
Whacko!	4th Oct.*
Lenny the Lion	19th Nov.*
1957	
The Benny Hill Show	5th Jan.*
Six-Five-Special	16th Feb.*
Tonight	18th Feb.*
On Safari	22nd Feb.*
Panorama	1st April*
The Sky at night	24th April*
Pinky and Perky	20th Oct.*
The Queen's Christmas Broadcast	25th Dec.*
1958	
Black and White Minstrel Show	14th June*
Grandstand	11th Oct.*
Blue Peter	16th Oct.*
1959	
Dixon of Dock Green	
What's My Line	
Sunday Night at the London Palladium	
Double Your Money	
Quatermass	
The Adventures of Robin Hood	
Sir Lancelot	
William Tell	
The Buccaneers	
The Count of Monte Cristo	
Sword of Freedom	
and many more.	

I think our first television set came from Janes & Adams in Shenley Road. It could have been a 20" rental. The other electrical shop was owned by Geo. D. Lilley who ran one of the original radio and television shops in Boreham Wood. His shop was on the corner of Shenley Road and Furzehill Road.

George Lilley was always advertising in the Boreham Wood & Elstree Post and other local news papers.

GEO.D.LILLEY

68 Shenley Road
Boreham Wood, Herts.

Phone: ELSTREE 1298
Established 1927

ONLY 49 GNS TAX PAID ONLY 49 GNS TAX PAID

Bush Television TV22

New technique provides increased picture area ease of operation and maximum suppression of interference.

AC OR DC

ONLY 49 GNS - TAX PAID

For Value - Sheer, down-to-earth value - There's nothing to challenge this Bush set. You get a good, clear picture-and you get it with the greatest of ease. You will appreciate at once the skill and experience that go to make this set possible-and make it such s sound investment. Look in at our showroom; Compare this Bush TV22 with anything else in view; and then-

LOOK AGAIN AT PRICE 49 GNS!
Tax Paid

Please ask your representative to call at:

NAME...

ADDRESS..

GEO. D. LILLEY
68 Shenley Road
Boreham Wood, Herts.
Phone : ELSTREE 1298
Established 1927

Sales Service Qualified Engineers. 48 Hour Repair Service. 3 Months Guarantee with All Work Estimates Free.	Bush Pye Decca Ultra Mullard Baird Marconi Ferguson Receivers and Records Etc., Etc.	House Wiring Points Immersion Heaters Fluorescent Fittings Washing Machines Refrigerators

THE MASTERS VOICE

The Hallmark of Quality

VISIT OUR SHOWS ROOMS
T E L E V I S I O N
Come and see Pye's new " Black Screen."

GEO.D.LILLEY
68 Shenley Road
Boreham Wood, Herts.
Phone: ELSTREE 1298
Established 1927

PYE MODEL VT4

THIS 14" TUBE WITH 13 CHANNELS

EXCELLENT FOR

BBC & COMMERCIAL TV

ONLY **67 GNS** (TAX PAID)

Geo. D. Lilley's adverts
in the
Boreham Wood & Elstree Post

1951–52

Fig 129.

1950s Television Nostalgia!

Adverts

Cadum Soap
Capstan Cigarettes
Esso Blue
Rowntree's Fruit Gums
Gibbs SR toothpaste
Murraymints
PG Tips
Rice Krispies
Tide
Strand Cigarettes

Adventure

The Black Arrow
The Buccaneers
The Count of Monte Cristo
Gun Smoke
Ivanhoe
Sergeant Bilko
Sir Francis Drake
Sir Lancelot
Lassie
Long John Silver
Robin Hood
The Scarlet Pimpernel
Sword of Freedom
The Gay Cavalier
Circus Boy
William Tell

Children's Programmes

Andy Pandy
Bengo
Bill & Ben
Billy Bunter
The Bumblies
Captain Pugwash
Cracker Jack
Hank

Ivor the Engine
Lenny the lion
Mr Pastry
Mr Turnip
Muffin the Mule
Noddy
Noggin
Pinky & Perky
Prudence
Pussy Cat William
Ragtail & Bobtail
Rolf Harris
Sooty
Twizzle
The Wooden Tops
Worzel Gummidge

Comedy

The Army Game
Arthur Askey
Arthur Haynes
Benny Hill
Dickie Henderson
Frankie Howard
Harry Worth
Jimmy Edwards
The Larkins
Mick & Montmorency
Tony Hancock

Drama

Dixon of Dock Green
Emergency Ward 10
The Invisible man

Family

The Appleyards
Amand & Michaela Dennis
The Grove Family

Game Shows

Criss Cross Quiz
Double Your Money
Spot the Tune
This is your life

Take Your Pick
What's my Line?

Pop Shows

Six Five Special

Science Fiction

Quatermass

TV Channels

ABC
Anglia
ATV
BBC
Granada
ITN
Rediffusion
Southern
TV Times

Variety

Billy Cotton
Black & White Minstrels
Sunday Night at the London Palladium

Westerns

Casey Jones
Champion the Wonder Horse
Cheyenne
The Cisco Kid
Davy Crockett
Flicka Hawkeye
Gun Smoke
The Lone Ranger
Maverick
Rawhide
Rin Tin Tin
Wagon Train
Zorro

More Memories of Boreham Wood in the 1950s

Home of Rest for Horses

I have fond memories of visiting *The Home of Rest for Horses* which once stood on the land of the present-day Farriers Way Estate. The home was initially based in Acton and moved to Cricklewood in 1908 and then it was transferred to Boreham Wood in 1933.

The charity was originally founded to give London's working horses, particularly those used by cab and delivery companies, the chance for rest and recuperation.

It was a very popular place to visit, especially at the weekends; sometimes my parents took us on a Sunday afternoon to see and treat the horses with sugar lumps!

The home had five separate fenced-off fields with 40 stables, surrounding a court yard which had a fountain and a pond containing goldfish and a large arched entrance off Furzehill Road.

There used to be a Georgian-style house, which was occupied by its chief executive and the groom; they lived in a flat at the entrance.

Sugar lumps, please!

Fig 130. [E.B.W.M.]

One of the stables had a bell fitted outside the door and every time someone was near, the horse inside would poke his head out and ring the bell; he would then expect you to give him some sugar lumps! The Boreham Wood buildings were demolished in September 1972 following the Home's move to Princes Risborough.

Going for a Picnic

I remember when we first moved to Boreham Wood in the early 1950s we made friends with our next door neighbours and we had many picnics together in Scratch Woods.

It was usually either on a weekend or whilst we were on our school holidays when our mums would get together to arrange the picnics.

We always looked forward to this occasion because it gave us a little bit more freedom to be able to run around, play our favourite games and explore the woods.

On the day our mothers would prepare some sandwiches. They usually contained jam, spam, cheese or corned-beef (you'd be lucky!). The mothers would take turns to make fairy cakes. Home made orange squash would wash it all down.

In those days it was far too expensive to own a car, but we didn't mind walking the mile south along the A1 to the Scratch Woods entrance.

Bird Spotting

It was towards the end of the late 1950s when I developed an interest in bird-spotting (the feathered variety!). Armed with my 1952 Observer Book of Birds and 1954 book of Birds Eggs, I started looking for birds by exploring the fields on the other side of the A1 Barnet-By-Pass, not far from where we lived. I had to cross this very busy road and then climb over a barbed wire fence, into the cow fields and then head in the direction of Rowley Lane. In those days we were still surrounded by plenty of open countryside. It was surprising how many rare birds I spotted that were mentioned in my bird book, to name just a few; Jay, Skylark, House Martin, Swift, Swallow, Green Woodpecker, Cuckoo, King Fisher, Barn Owl, Little Owl, Tawny Owl, Sparrow Hawk, Kestrel, Wren, Lapwing and many more. Today, it's sad to have to say that many of these lovely creatures are no longer flying around in the fields that I mentioned.

Train Spotting

British Railways Passenger Express heading for St. Pancras, hauled by ex-LMS Rebuilt "Royal Scot" Class Locomotive

Taken by the Brick Fields 1959.

Fig 131. [V.R.]

Train spotting in the 1950s was an interesting and exciting time for many of the teenagers of Boreham Wood who just couldn't wait to get down to the station and fill in their little books.

I can proudly say that I was one of those teenagers who did exactly that. This was one of my hobbies that didn't cost me much money; unlike today's play-stations! All I needed was 2/6d (12.5p) which was my pocket money so I could buy a *Red Rover*, the equivalent of today's travel card. With that I could travel on buses and underground trains all over London and visit other main train stations to get train numbers for other regions.

Christmas Time

I shall always have fond memories of Christmas time in Boreham Wood in the 1950s, especially when I was young.

Our first Christmas living at 1, Knebworth Path in December 1952 was very simple because we had not long moved into our new home. We hardly had any furniture and there were no carpets on the floors, only some cheap lino which felt cold, especially in winter time.

The house had no central heating, only a coal fire in the living room, which ate up the coal like nobody's business! This fire would also heat the upstairs airing cupboard hot water cylinder which also had an immersion heater that we could use if there wasn't enough hot water from the coal fire.

On some very cold and frosty winter nights, my mother used to carefully fill an empty Tizer bottle with hot water and place it in our beds. (i.e. we had no hot water bottle!)

When I woke in the morning and looked out of the bedroom window I had a real surprise, the window was just thick ice, making it very difficult to see what was going on outside. The only way to clear this was to breathe on the ice and make a circle with my hands, finishing up with a small porthole to look through!

On Christmas Eve Mum would be busy in the kitchen making some mince pies and Dad would be out trying to buy a Christmas tree.

As the day got darker, mum would put some more coal on the fire trying to keep the sitting room nice and warm. I would sit on a chair making paper chains. I hated the taste of the glue! I used to get excited thinking about the presents Father Christmas might bring me.

Eventually Dad would arrive home with a real Christmas tree that he had probably bought somewhere in the Village. It was usually about 4ft high and very bushy. Apparently my mother always insisted for some reason on having a bushy one!

Our next performance involved decorating the tree. We had to use real candles because we couldn't afford to buy electric lights, although we once bought some for the following Christmas. We added tinsel and some coloured glass balls before finally placing a little fairy on the top.

As a child I thought the Christmas tree always looked pretty; especially after Dad lit the candles; the whole tree came to life and the balls were shining!

After all this hard work it was bath time and then to bed; and this was where I had difficulty in trying to sleep. It's a well known fact that every child at this time of year goes through the same experience, tossing and turning and trying to work out what presents they were going to get for Christmas.

On Christmas morning, not having had much sleep, I couldn't wait to check my Christmas stocking. This was just as exciting as getting my main presents. Inside the stocking, without fail there were always a couple of walnuts, an orange, apple and some chocolates or sweets.

Mum and Dad would still be in bed sound asleep probably worn out from the night before wrapping all the presents!

It was only 5 o'clock in the morning and all I wanted to do was get up and go downstairs to see what presents Father Christmas had left.

There was always a warning from my parents who said that if I went downstairs to the sitting room before they went down, I would get *gold-fingers* if I opened the door to try to see my presents. If this was true by now I would be a very rich man! I had to sit and freeze in my bedroom and wait until they had risen and gone downstairs when they would call me.

When they eventually got up, Dad went downstairs to light the fire and Mother told me that I could go downstairs and stand in the kitchen and wait until the water pipes heated up. These pipes came down the wall from the airing cupboard and into the back of the fire. As soon as this happened my mother said I could go in and see my presents.

When I walked into the sitting room I saw that my father had lit the candles on the Christmas tree and the fire would be blazing away; it looked very festive.

My father always cooked the Christmas dinner and we all sat around the table listening to the radio; there was no television and no Queens's speech.

Inside the Christmas pudding there was always a *Thruppenny Bit*. I had to be very careful not to swallow it!

A Silver *Thruppenny* Bit

Fig 132. [V.R.]

In the afternoon, Dad would normally fall asleep in the armchair, Mum would be cracking nuts and I happily played with my Christmas presents.

As I grew older my presents got more exciting. One year I had a Tri-Ang train set; it was a blue double-ended American diesel which had working lights on each end of the front of the engine; it also had very attractive carriages with seats on the top enclosed in a clear plastic canopy.

On another occasion I had my first *Raleigh* bicycle; the brakes had iron rods and not cables like the bikes of today.

Timeline of Events

Public Houses

In the 1950s there were already some pubs in Boreham Wood.

The King's Arms; at Stirling Corner, now a Harvester Restaurant

The Elstree Way Hotel, Elstree Way, no longer there

The Red Lion, Shenley Road, now McDonalds

The Crown, Shenley Road

The Wellington, Theobald Street.

During the 1950s we saw the building of many new pubs in the area.

The Bull & Tiger, in Ripon Way, now the Directors
Arms, opened its doors on 6th July 1955

The Suffolk Punch, later the Willow Tree in Howard Drive,
opened its doors in 1957, demolished by 2010

The Green Dragon, in Leeming Road

The Shooting Star, in Rossington Avenue

The Cannon, in Thirsk Road

The Wood Cock, in Barton Way, demolished

The King's Arms
at Stirling Corner
1950s

Fig 133. [D.A.]

In *January 1952* it was proposed to build a new Fire and Ambulance station in the Elstree Way. Meanwhile a building in Manor Way was being temporarily used until the new premises became available. The building was originally designed as a factory which would have to be returned to its owners.

June 1952. Shoppers calling in for an early morning cup of coffee at the Dutch Oven in Shenley Road were surprised to hear an ingenious talking model baker-man in the shop. The model was an electrically operated ventriloquist dummy. Lip and face movements were synchronized with the sound which came from concealed records.

October 1952. Boreham Wood's first Santa Claus was already in sight – the Village Hall, Shenley Road was booked for the first Christmas exhibition and festivities, which made early offers of economical family Christmas presents. Running for four days, November 18 to 21, the Christmas Sale was graced by the first seasonal Father Christmas together with a traditional lucky dip.

Although the sale had been planned by local trader Mr. George Lilley, the centre-piece of it all, the jovial, red-cheeked Santa with his flowing beard and locks and scarlet gown had not yet appeared.

Mr. Lilley told the Boreham Wood & Elstree Post he was confident of finding an early Santa, saving the kiddies the disappointment of a non-appearance. (Any volunteers!)

February 1953. A *Rag & Bone* man from Sandal Street, West Ham was summoned under the Public Health Act at Barnet Sessions and was fined a total of £3.

He was alleged to have given a packet of Plasticine to a child under 14 while he was collecting rags in Arundel Drive Boreham Wood and to have given a picture book to two other children at the same time and place.

The Clerk from Elstree Rural District Council said that he had been standing by his van receiving small bundles of rags from young children, for which he gave them packets of plasticine or picture books. He had been warned previously not to commit the offence.

The arresting Police Officer said that when he told the man about the offence, he said that he did not know that he was doing any harm. He said that he did go to the houses to get the rags, but the parents prefer to send their children to him. He then pleaded guilty.

July 1953. Approval was given by Hertfordshire County Council for Boreham Wood to have a new Fire and Ambulance station costing about £22,900 to be built on a site in the Elstree Way.

The Fire Brigade Committee reported that the present Fire and Ambulance Station occupied premises leased from Laing's Properties Ltd., at an exclusive rent of £1000 a year.

Having regard to the high rent charged, the committee was of the opinion that a new Fire station should be built as soon as possible.

The original premises of the
Boreham Wood Fire Services
in Manor Way
in 2009.

This building was used in 1953.

Fig 134. [V.R.]

The completed Fire &
Ambulance Station
in the Elstree Way
c1954/5

Fig 135. [B.W.L.]

The Boreham Wood Library
in 1958

Fig 136. [B.W.L.]

November 1953. It was proposed to build a new library in the Elstree Way at a cost of £9000. The library was opened in 1957.

May 1954. Advertisements in the Boreham Wood & Elstree Post cost 2d (less than 1p) per word for three insertions

May 1954. The War Memorial was moved from the southern end of Theobald Street to a new position outside the Red Lion pub, now McDonald's, in Shenley Road.

July 1954. The Day Nursery in Shenley Road was closed after Christmas. John Laing Ltd.. had requested the nursery to vacate the premises to allow new development including a store for Woolworths. The Day Nursery accommodated about 80 children.

September 1954. A meeting was held to decide the future of the *Three-Ways-Community-Centre* based on the three roads: Ripon Way, Manor Way and Cranes Way.

October 1954. Princes Margaret laid a foundation stone at St. Michael's Church in Brook/ Gateshead Road.

October 1954. Teddy Boys were refused admission to a local dance hall. Fireworks were set off in the Studio Cinema in Shenley Road.

July 1955. Thieves broke into High Canons and stole some cash. Two thieves were questioned about the incident.

August 1955. The construction of a new Police Station in the Elstree Way was approved. The planned opening date of February 1957 was delayed and it opened the 4th March 1957.

August 1955. Foxes were on the prowl in Boreham Wood when twenty-five chickens were killed in one night! Local residents were warned that even if they didn't keep chickens, cats could also be victims.

March 1956. A new tower for the All Saints Church in Shenley Road was proposed. It was built in 1958.

February 1957. The brewers Charring & Co. proposed to build a new pub, the *Suffolk Punch,* in Howard Drive/Balmoral Drive.

May 1957. A new Family Clinic opened in the Elstree Way.

May 1957. 107 & 306 Buses began a service in Balmoral Drive.

August 1957. Plans submitted for new building at Elliott Brothers (London) Ltd. in the Elstree Way.

November 1957. The introduction of Red-Rovers, a new travel card bargain costing 5/- (25p) for adults and 2/6d (12.5p) for children.

February 1958. Previously Shenley Road had grass banks running along both sides of the high street, but in 1958 the County Council decided to widen the road, to make it more accessible.

Widening the road started in November 1957, but by February 1958 the work had ground to a halt, while telephone, gas and electric companies re-laid their cables in the road. There was a lot of snow on the ground, which made working very difficult..

The Shenley Road shopkeepers were annoyed about the building site because their customers had to walk past the works to go shopping. They threatened to stop paying their rates. The Hertfordshire County Council responded by apologising, and blamed the utility companies for the disruption.

September 1958. My father was working as a bar steward in the *Kings Arms* pub at Stirling Corner. One night, after work, he walked home along his regular route by the service road next to the A1 Barnet By-Pass and when he arrived home, my mother was waiting to open the door for him. I was still awake and I can still remember him coming home looking rather shocked, frightened and shaking like mad! Mum was trying to ask him what was wrong, and I then heard him say *"I've just seen a ghost!"*

In the same month a local newspaper published this article; *"Is there a ghost at Stirling Corner?"* Mysterious woman who smiles and vanishes at Stirling Corner – experienced by a local man who said that he heard a noise and went to investigate, he saw a woman standing near a derelict shed. He looked around to see if anyone else was nearby, looked back, and to use his own words *"There she was, gone!"*

Final Memories

Sunday School
Church Lads Brigade
Sea Cadets
Nature walks
Youth clubs
Cycling
Talent contests
Hopscotch
The Daily Mirror
The Beano
The Dandy
The Topper
The Beezer
Conkers
Dinky Toys
Fireworks and bonfire night
Marbles
Match Box Toys
Smiths Crisps with the little blue bag of salt
Gob stoppers
Sweet tobacco
Black jacks
Aniseed balls
Bread pudding
Fish cakes
Spam fritters and chips fried in lard
Custard and steam pudding
Sugar sandwiches bread and jam
Full cooked English breakfast
Sunday roast dinner
Stew
Traditional salad with real salad cream
Jelly and ice cream
The cane
Courting
The dentists drill!

Part Two

The Developers' Story

The following pages describe the transformation of Boreham Wood as a village to its status as a town by the 1960s.

Development of the new estates was far from trouble-free. Some of the problems faced by the developers during the early years of the 1950s are described.

pre-1950s Boreham Wood

The area was originally mostly farmland, village life being centred around Theobald Street where artisans and servants provided services to the small community and to Elstree Village. Growth on a significant scale came when the LMS Railway opened in 1868 and a station and sidings were constructed. By the start of the 20th Century there were thriving manufacturing businesses in the area, notably Wellington and Ward's Photographic Works, which prompted the construction of shops and houses. Thus Shenley Road and Drayton Road began to be developed. A steady increase in the number of businesses, houses and shops continued until after the First World War.

After the First World War the expansion of London's suburbs and its satellite Garden Cities went ahead regardless of the great economic difficulties in Britain. Boreham Wood grew as it was able to provide employment to migrant workers in factories such as the Keystone Knitting Mills and the emerging entertainment industry which needed studios to produce films for cinemas which were being built all over the country. Construction of the A1 Barnet By-pass in 1928 was a further impetus to growth. The 1930s saw the development of Whitehouse Avenue, Cardinal Avenue, Grosvenor Road and parades of shops in Shenley Road, which were very convenient for the studios' employees as well as local residents. Small to medium sized blocks of houses sprang up in such roads as those leading off Furzehill Road.

Before the Second Word War the construction company, John Laing and Sons, proposed and laid out a large area of land next to the A1 for their Elstree Garden City, which was to be built along the lines of Letchworth Garden City. The company built many factories that played an essential role during the Second World War and made a significant start on the construction of nearby houses.

Boreham Wood's studios, factories and buildings hosted the war effort in various ways, including the following examples. The A.B.P.C Studio was a vast store for materials, including decoys, that helped in the invasion of Europe on D-Day. The Studio also hosted the Garrison Theatre. An activity carried out in the Amagamated Studios, later M.G.M. Studios, was the construction of aeroplane parts for Halifax bombers. Other aeroplane and vehicle parts were made in Laing's factories along the Elstree Way and A1, such as the Henderson Safety Tank Company and Opperman's. Government ministries moved records to the town for safer storage. Smaller companies such as Keystone Knitting Mills turned to war work and the prestigious road-house known as the Thatched Barn secretly housed a branch of S.O.E. that dealt in camouflage and the training of secret agents. A local hairdresser even gave his services to groom agents before their mission.

After the War Laing's continued to develop and convert its industrial units in the area, as well as shops and public buildings. Adhesive Tapes Ltd. required several sites. Elliott Brothers, which started its Boreham Wood branch in 1949 eventually required a large site in Elstree Way to develop and build defence equipment and computers.

Laing's factory designs have a characteristic appearance. They have a brick facade with a square central or corner square tower which hides a steel-framed shop-floor.

Fig 137. [E.B.W.M.] Laing's HQ Building

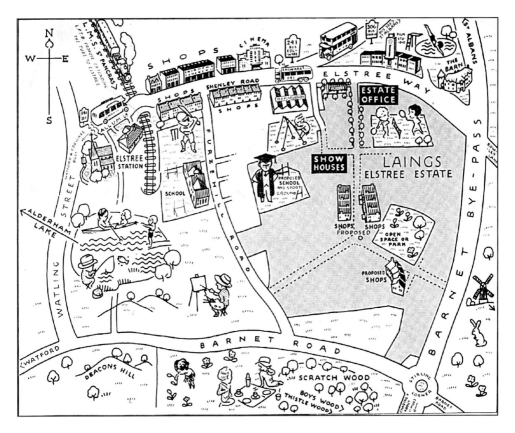

Fig 138. [E.B.W.M.] Laing's pre-War Plan for a model garden city

Elstree Rural District Council
(previously Barnet Rural District Council)

The Elstree Rural District Council began a programme of council house building. In 1944 about 50 German prisoners of war were drafted in from a nearby camp in Station Road to begin the building work. As an emergency measure, caravans were parked both sides of the A1 at Stirling Corner.

Caravans at Stirling Corner
Fig 139. [E.B.W.M.]

Emergency housing, in the form of **prefabs** was built in Eldon Avenue, while caravan accommodation, still present, was popular on a site near Stirling Corner. In 1949 they had completed their 500th council house.

Prefabs in Eldon Avenue
Shenley Road with the A.B.P.C. Studios in the foreground
and the National Studios centre left. Fields in the background.

Fig 140. [E.B.W.M.]

London County Council (L.C.C)

After the Second World War, Boreham Wood was chosen as one of the Labour Government's new housing developments. The compulsory purchase of farm land both north and south of Elstree Way provided the space for new housing. What happened in Boreham Wood, as far as building was concerned, can be seen from the L.C.C. house building programme of the 1950s. You will see they encountered problems which were mainly caused by the workers' dissatisfaction.

The following time plan describes what happened, especially on the No. 2 housing estate.

In the late 1940s the L.C.C. (London County Council) started negotiations with the County Councils for the possibility of using some of the land in the counties. Boreham Wood was chosen for one of their developments of new housing estates.

In September 1949 contracts were signed and permission was granted for the erection of new and traditional council houses, which could take about three years to complete. These would eventually house about 15,000 people. The cost of the estate would be over £7,000,000.

Although the plans were ready and approved, the exact date when work on the new L.C.C. estates would commence was unknown. According to the County Council, the first builders and carpenters could move in within a few months and all they needed was the signal to *Go!*

Other records around at the time stated they were going to build 4080 houses on the Boreham Wood Estate in the years 1950-100, 1951-550, 1952-1200, 1953 -1200, 1954-1030. These figures were later extended.

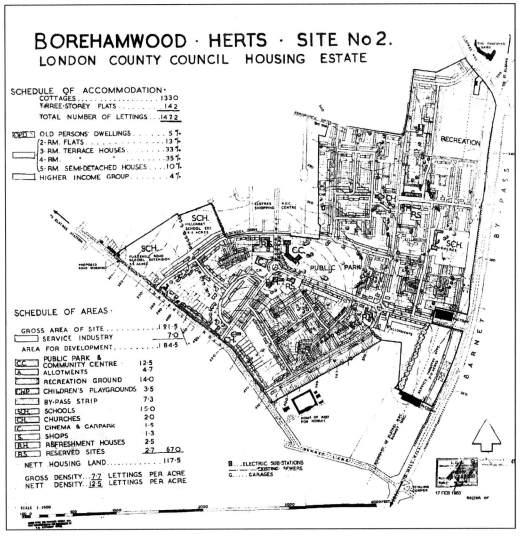

Fig 141. [E.B.W.M.] L.C.C. Plan of 1950 Site No 2

The London building contractors, Gee, Walker, Slater, were given the contract to build the new houses. They had to employ many bricklayers, plumbers, carpenters, electricians and labourers for the undertaking.

The development was to be in two complete neighbourhood units, the No. 1 site would be bounded by Theobald Street and Cowley Hill, and the number No. 2 site was to be on the west side of the A1 Barnet-by-pass, commencing south of the Thatched Barn and finishing just north of Stirling Corner and would be bounded by Elstree Way and Furzehill Road and as far as the Home of Rest for Horses, facing south. The No. 2 site was to be undertaken first.

L.C.C.. No. 2 Building Site
Cranes Way c1950

Fig 142. [D.A.]

Tenants for the dwellings on the L.C.C. housing estate at Boreham Wood were to be selected from the applicants on the L.C.C.'s 1949 housing list.

There were to be many different styles of houses and flats for the tenants to choose from. One, two, three and four bedroom houses and some one and two bedroom flats and not forgetting the *old folk* bungalows. The majority of these would be built using traditional bricks, but included among them were ninety-six concrete houses. Also scheduled were some houses, believe it or not, that were made from plywood!

One of the L.C.C. officials had described them as being **very attractive**. The average cost of each house would be around £1,700 each. It should be noted that by 1950 there were around 161,000 people on the L.C.C.'s housing list.

By February 1950 the London County Council scheme was well under way.

L.C.C.. No. 2 Building Site
Cranes Way c1950

Fig 143. [D.A.]

In March 1950 there occurred the first phase of many troubles to hit the L.C.C.'s No.2 building site where they had a serious shortage of skilled bricklayers. The London contractors, who had just begun the work on the **Ripon Way** estate, said *"We only have nine skilled bricklayers on the site and we need over fifty immediately"*. The main cause of the shortage was that most of their labour force came from Central London but too many people who were seeking work said that Boreham Wood sounded too remote and isolated.

In April 1950 the contractors advertised the excellent tube service running from London to Burnt Oak, saying *"We will pick up the workers in their trucks each day and take them directly to the different building sites where they will find excellent canteen facilities and get a hot lunch and cup of tea for 1s. 4½d."* (under 7p)

The company also looked into the possibility of offering employment to about 250 Polish workers who were living in the hostel camp of Nissen Huts in Theobald Street, Boreham Wood; the hostel was scheduled to be closed on the 4th June 1950.

The company announced they were offering **limitless bonuses**. They said *"We are paying £5 bonuses to our bricklayers, who can earn as much as £15 or £16 in bonuses a week"*; they added *"the more men they get the bigger bonuses they can pay".*

Reports that the bricklayers were receiving £16 in bonuses a week, a lot of money in those days, on the L.C.C. Housing estates were refuted by the men's union. The reports followed those of a severe shortage of labour.

Exhaustive enquiries made by a local newspaper at the time produced the following findings:

1 There had been a slight shortage of labour because many workers on the site had to travel over an hour to work.

2 In the initial stages of all projects there are *growing pains* but as employees are offered a fairly long security of tenure, these are overcome.

3 The workers were earning nowhere near the £16 bonuses suggested.

An official of the Amalgamated Union of Building Trade Workers said *"There probably had been a shortage of workers but if conditions are good we think the contractors could employ all the workers they need."*

At the time a member of the London Divisional Council of the Union said *"The highest bonus paid on the Boreham Wood site is £3.12s"*, (£3.60p). *"To earn £16 a week bonus, each man would have to lay a minimum of 2,400 bricks a day, which would be most remarkable for the type of work."*

There was a scarcity of labour in the immediate vicinity of the site because of the travelling distance, but this was being overcome by special travelling arrangements.

During the month of April 1950 a local reporter visited the L.C.C. site and reported

"I found it a hive of activity. The bricklayers were busy working on the new houses, many of which were not far off completion. Offices and huts where the labourers can relax during the lunch hour have been erected on the site. There were piles of bricks, pipes, scaffolding and other building materials lying near the houses and not one of the men was sitting around doing nothing; all were doing one job or another. There appeared to be no shortage of workmen. Lorries were continuously arriving, bringing materials and other vehicles were on the spot."

In the same month there began the first of numerous serious strikes which were to be experienced on the L.C.C.'s building sites. The dismissal of two carpenters who were working on the No.2 site caused a *lightning strike* by seventeen other carpenters over a weekend, but the men resumed work at the beginning of the following week.

In May 1950 further labour problems on the L.C.C.'s 5,000 home Boreham Wood housing estate reached a climax when thirty-two bricklayers on the site were dismissed by the contractors, Messrs. Gee, Walker and Slater, who alleged that they had been *going slow* throughout the week. Several of them were members of the Amalgamated Union of Building Trades Workers, who were picketing the site since the dismissals. At the time a union official who organised the picketing told the firm that the union consider the firm's action constituted a *lock-out*.

A firm's spokesman commenting on the dismissals told a local reporter that there had been two lightning strikes after the discharge of two carpenters and several half-hour stoppages because of the bonus scheme which the men consider compares unfavourably with those on the other L.C.C. Housing sites. He alleged that the trouble had begun because of *Communist elements* among the bricklayers, who were using the bonus scheme as an excuse to stir unrest.

Work had already begun on 100 of the 5,000 houses planned but the firm did not employ any more bricklayers until the findings of the disputes committee were published, to which both sides made their case known.

The firm also said *"there is enough work in hand to keep the remaining tradesmen and labours employed for some time."*

The men claimed *"we are not going slow, but working to rule."* One of the bricklayers concerned, who was a member of the *Communist Party* and chairman of the committee representing the workers on the site, described the firm's accusation that they, the communists, were the cause of the trouble as absolute nonsense! One of the other bricklayers, who was also a communist candidate in Bethnal Green in a general election, said *"you will always find among any group of workers, communists and members of other political parties. It is so easy to describe any action with which you do not agree as communist inspired."*

Another bricklayer, who was among the pickets, said that he was a Labour man and did not care what party the union officials belonged to. He was only interested in settling the dispute and getting back to work. At the time they were only being paid the Union's 25s (£1.25p) a week lock-out money.

One of the firm's decorators and sign writers revealed that communist sympathisers among the men had little backing from their colleagues, most of whom considered they were *getting a fair crack of the whip!*

Two weeks later the labour dispute on the L.C.C. estate was still unsettled and developed into a two-way hassle over the re-employment of one of the thirty-two bricklayers who were dismissed because he was a communist candidate for Bethnal Green in a general election. The remaining bricklayers were given the chance of returning to their work but they refused because the contractors would not let their colleague return to work because of his political beliefs.

During a meeting of 150 of the other workers, nearly all the remaining men on the site decided they would down tools if he was reinstated. Remember, that the thirty-two bricklayers were originally discharged after a dispute over the bonus scheme operated by the contractors.

The Disputes Commission deplored the fact that a serious situation had been allowed to develop before either the firm or the unions had consulted the conciliation machinery and recommended that the men should apply for re-employment and that the firm should reinstate them.

In the same week both sides and about eight of the bricklayers reported back to work while others found employment elsewhere. The firm said *"We are willing to take all these men back except for the trouble maker"*, but the men said *"We are not prepared to go back without him,"* so they immediately downed tools and posted pickets on the site.

Both sides later put their case to another Disputes Commission saying that the men should be reinstated and recommended that the *trouble maker* be employed on the firm's site at Hanover Square in London for three weeks, after which the question of his return to Boreham Wood be reviewed.

Just before the second commission sat, the other workers on the site met and issued their ultimatum saying *"We will not work with the trouble maker"*.

One of the loading gangers, who organised the meeting, told a local newspaper reporter *"While we are not working we are losing money and cannot earn any bonuses or overtime."*

He also said they had little sympathy with the bricklayers because of the political capital that had been made of the trouble. They believed the firm were giving them a *square deal.*

An official from the firm denied the bricklayers' accusations that they were victimising the *trouble maker* and said *"We don't care about the man's political colour or creed, so long as his expressions of political belief do not cause a disturbance at his work"*. He emphasised that the firm were willing to take back all the bricklayers, including those who had found work since being dismissed and said they were welcome to come back when the trouble had blown over. In the case of the *trouble maker* the firm would abide by the Commission's recommendation that he should be offered work on the Hanover Square site until his position could be reviewed.

Towards the end of **May 1950** there seemed to be no end to the building site disputes; they just didn't want to go away. A meeting was held with 200 workers on the L.C.C. housing site at Ripon Way which included plumbers, carpenters, plasterers, scaffold workers and labourers. They told the contractors, Gee Walker Slater, that they refused to work with the thirty-two bricklayers on the site because of all the trouble and strikes they had caused.

The *lightning strike* in April that was about the dismissals of two carpenters was repeated a month later when the workers downed tools and caused a second *lightning strike!* The bricklayers, carpenters, labourers and other men were protesting because no decision had been reached regarding the dismissals, which they claim at the time were unjustified.

A twenty-nine-year-old bricklayer and chairman of the committee which represented the workers on the site, told a local newspaper that the employers, Messrs. Gee, Walker and Slater refused to discuss the matter until the strike, which involved about eighty men, ended. The men did however return to work only because their representatives started re-negotiations with the employers for the reinstatement of the carpenters and if the firm refused to re-employ the men, the case would go to a disputes committee.

The men were considering sending a deputation to the L.C.C. to complain about the organisation on the site, alleging general dissatisfaction among the men about the firm's bonus scheme. It was said that when the work began a few months ago, the firm decided to give the men an incentive and issued target figures for the time each job should take, but the targets were about thirty per cent, lower than other L.C.C. housing sites.

He claimed that the men had less chance of earning bonuses and when the men suggested the alterations, the firm agreed to only trivial adjustments. The men therefore refused to work the bonus scheme.

In June 1950 after weeks of disputes and strikes, the bricklayers were back at work on the 5,000 home L.C.C.'s housing estate but the bonus scheme over which the trouble began remained unaltered.

Both sides were standing their ground over the scheme. The bricklayers refused to work it. The contractors, Messrs. Gee, Walker and Slater, were not prepared to alter it. Negotiations were continuing.

A bricklayers' spokesman told the local press

"We fully appreciate the position of London's homeless who want these houses, but we don't see why we should work a bonus scheme which compares unfavourably with those on other L.C.C. Sites. We will do a normal day's work and no more. But", they said, *"we are not planning any more strikes!"*

June 1950 Gee, Walker, Slater, the building contractors for the L.C.C. housing estate at Ripon Way, took over the former Polish camp in Theobald Street as quarters for the workmen on the estate. One hundred and eighty were to be accommodated at the camp and brought from the North of England and the Midlands, though sixty of them were Poles who had transferred from local factories to work for the contractors.

The remaining 60 out of 120 Poles who formerly occupied the camp had moved out of the district, although a few had found local accommodation.

By February 1951 two thirds of the road and sewer work had been completed on the L.C.C.'s No.2 housing estate yielding some positive results.

At the end of the month the local newspapers announced *"The first of the 15,000 Londoners would move into their new homes on Thursday 1 March 1951 as tenants on the L.C.C.'s new Boreham Wood housing estate in Ripon Way."*

On Thursday 1ˢᵗ March 1951 the first family took possession of their new home, they had two children, a girl aged six and a boy aged four. They came from a dark and damp two-room basement in a rebuilt blitzed house in Julian Street, Kilburn where they had lived since 1944. Their old house had no bathroom and the family used a tin bath in the living room.

The L.C.C.'s Director of Housing had suggested that the manufactures and Council should welcome them and let them know they were part of the new community and expect them to become loyal citizens. But on the day of their arrival there were no speeches, no flags and no welcome letters from the Elstree Rural District Council. The arrival of the vanguard was unspectacular. A pantechnicon loaded with furniture rolled up to *62 Ripon Way*, near the A1. Barnet By-Pass and the family from Kilburn had arrived.

The workmen on the site were too busy with their own troubles to give the new arrivals more than a second glance and Boreham Wood itself slumbered on as though nothing was happening. Yet it was the beginning of a process that would nearly treble the area's population.

A local reporter who was on the site said he was made very welcome by the family who had invited him into their new home and gave him a conducted tour, showing him their very large living room recess and well equipped kitchen. The family explained to the reporter *"It is like a palace after the basement we have been living in."*

New residents compare their old and new homes

Fig 144 [E.B.W.M.]

On Friday 2nd **March 1951** the second family arrived and moved in next door to join their new neighbours. They, like the first family, had been living in two rooms with their two children, a girl aged eight and a boy aged four. They had lived in Finsbury Park for five years.

On Saturday 3rd **March 1951** the third family moved into their new four-bedroom house with their five sons and 26 year-old invalid daughter. It was the first time for six years that they could have her with them because she had been injured in a car crash during the war as an A.T.S. radar operator at Lowestoft. She was paralysed from the waist down.

Some of the first new residents moving to Boreham Wood

Fig 145 [E.B.W.M.]

The most striking things about Ripon Way in those days were the mud, cranes, tractors, lorries, jeeps, piles of bricks and other materials, the half-built houses and the clothes of the workmen.

Despite all the mess and inconvenience caused by the building project, the planners had hopes and visions of Boreham Wood being a very attractive residential neighbourhood, including houses for what were described officially as **managerial class.** It would be liberally sprinkled with open spaces and children's playgrounds.

There were to be some **old-folk's dwellings** grouped around a park and one building would provide the old people with a **Darby and Joan Club,** reading room and library. A community centre was also planned for the park. Eventually, the site could have its own cinema, (what cinema?) church and public house. But these amenities were very much something for the future as houses and shops were the first priority, the churches and public houses came last.

A mother of four children, like many of her neighbours, said *"It's difficult to get used to the isolation of our new home. When I come in from the street and shut the door, it feels very lonely. It's very different from Holloway Road where we used to live."*

The only serious criticism and concern about the houses was that the fire for heating water was in the living room rather than in the kitchen. According to one woman, a large amount of fuel was consumed. She said *"I've used 10 cwt of coal in a very short space of time."*

Some houses that had been completed in Grantham Green were eventually occupied and there were more still being built. The windows in some of the unoccupied houses had been broken and despite the optimistic title of the road there was not a vestige of green grass to be seen!

One of the new tenants from Grantham Green said there were heavy lumps of clay in her front garden, dug over by her husband and that her garden was now worse. The soil was so heavy that it was difficult to know what to do with it.

April 1951 brought good news for everyone working on the L.C.C.'s Ripon Way building estate, the long running dispute among the workers finally being settled. Just to recap, the trouble began sometime ago, when two carpenters were dismissed, because the contractors, Messrs. Gee, Walker and Slater Ltd., claimed a redundancy, owing to the failure of the subcontractors to adequately provide sufficient roofing tiles on the site. The other workers on the estate objected on the grounds that the dismissals were unnecessary.

The lack of roofing tilers caused a general delay in building. No rooves could be completed and it was, in consequence, not possible to finish the internal fixing of floors, erect slabbing or complete plastering. In the words of one of the stewards on the site *"a bottleneck exists! "*

Once again the men on the job objected, demanding that the dispute be settled. It was discovered that the tiling workers were not satisfied with their working conditions and they refused to stay on the job, to express their dissatisfaction. It was subsequently discovered that the tilers were employed on piece work at satisfactory wages.

The London County Council did not allow piece work on their housing estates, as they claimed that it lead to shoddy workmanship. At a meeting between Gee, Walker and

Slater representatives, the roofing subcontractors and the site steward, the subcontractors agreed to correct the position in regard to piece work. They also agreed to re-employ the workers under corrections and conditions and rates of pay. In a final statement the steward said that it had lead to a position in which the men enjoy an increase of wages.

Politicians opening a new housing estate in Boreham Wood. c1949

Fig 146   [E.B.W.M.]

In May 1951 work began on No 1 Site

The local newspapers announced that the contractors were preparing to start on the No.1 site in Theobald Street where some old farm buildings had to be demolished or converted into garages in preparation for constructional work. Preliminary levelling of the ground had already been undertaken on the site where it was planned to construct about 2,500 houses.

In June 1951 fifty houses and two-thirds of the roads and sewer work were completed on the *No. 2* L.C.C. Ripon Way housing estate, with 550 still under construction and another 900 to be started. The site was expected to be finished in late 1952, or at the beginning of 1953.

The construction of the houses were of the traditional brick style and it was planned to have about 100 concrete houses. These were made by the *no-fines* method of shuttering in which concrete containing hardly any sand or fine aggregate was moulded between wooden boards. This method was easily mechanised and reduced the number of bricklayers needed, an important factor to consider in those days of manpower shortage.

At the Ripon Way site, the dispute between the carpenters and the employers, Messrs. Gee, Walker and Slater Ltd. was settled. The men returned to work following their strike, when the employers offered them various advances to the bonus scheme. The men got a larger bonus for time saved on the job, which increased their bonus by 25 per cent. The employers also agreed to a bonus scheme for work covering only part of the week. This was, according to an official on the site, a substantial improvement for the carpenters, who were given an increase in their bonus rate of 5s (25p) per week. He added that the production at the site should return to a high level in about a week.

In September 1951, an L.C.C. official told a local newspaper *"104 houses have been completed on the No. 1 housing site and a further 800 are in the course of construction."*

In November 1951, another serious strike hit the Ripon Way housing estate when over

900 building workers engaged by Messrs. Gee, Walker and Slater Ltd. went on strike, demanding the reinstatement of four men (two stewards and two charge hands) sacked for refusing to operate to a target, the honouring of bonus agreements and provision of adequate shelters around the site. The strike committee stated that they would not return to work until their conditions were met and said that the employers have been complaining about *phenomenal bonuses* earned by men unloading lorries.

Pickets prevented work on the site and a meeting was arranged with the *Associated Union of Building Trade Disputes Committee.*

The weekly average of 17 houses being built was halted by the strike. Officials of the employers had no comment to make about the situation.

January 1952. A works canteen hut belonging to the building contractors Gee, Walker & Slater was used as a church in Ripon Way; this was on the new L.C.C. housing estate. In the same year they held a party for over 150 children.

In February 1952, somehow, according to my research, the workers on the L.C.C. Ripon Way housing estate struck for a week because 14 civil engineers were made redundant, but they had decided to return to work.

The men's spokesman said that all the men with the exception of 14 dismissed men, resumed work, on the employers' promise that the 14 men would be given jobs. They were to be given the first vacancies and would be provided with alternative work until then. The men on the job decided that while the 14 men were out of work, they would not operate the incentive bonus scheme. The employers called this *going slow*. After further negotiations they were told that the men would be taken back at the beginning of the week. After a mass meeting the men accepted the employers' promise and resumed the incentive bonus scheme.

Of the 14 dismissed men, two had changed their jobs and the remaining 12 returned to work on the site. An L.C.C. official said that the men were back at work and the situation seemed to have returned to normal. Some of the men who were declared redundant had been taken back by the contractors and other work found for them.

In March 1952, a meeting of 700 builders working on the Ripon Way estate accused the contractor of inefficiency in running the site. The meeting was convened to protest against publicity given to the workers on the site and particular to a leading article which appeared in a national newspaper.

The chairman of the meeting, who was a stewards' convenor and a member of the *National Federation of Building Trades Operatives,* claimed that the firm were causing the hold-ups and bottlenecks on the job by cutting down on the services. He strongly denied the allegations made by the Press that the strikes had been agitated by communists. He said that all the trouble had been caused by wilful and provocative attacks by the employers on trades-unionists and claimed that the strikes had been caused because the men had not been given proper targets at which to aim, and because of unnecessary dismissals. To sum it up, there were too many foremen on the job, who, instead of supervising properly, spent their time going round on bicycles collecting bits and pieces for the job. He explained that on one occasion the plumbers had to strike in order to get supplies delivered, to earn proper bonuses. To cut down on bonuses was to cut down on production.

Further accusations were made against the firm's inefficiency when it was alleged that nearly 100 of the new houses had been left derelict because of the severe winter frost, and there was a danger that when the thaw came, the water pipes could burst if left unattended for too long. An official from the firm said that the water was left on in the houses on the instructions of the L.C.C. because it was thought that the tenants would be moving in. It was true that the houses could be damaged after the frosts and they welcomed an enquiry into the running of the site. He also agreed that the public were entitled to know what the firm was up to.

In **August 1952**, there occurred what I believe was one of the worst news reports about the L.C.C.'s house building programme, which highlighted problems for both builders and thousands of families who were awaiting the completion of their new home.

The L.C.C. made a surprise announcement that it was closing down its £7,000,000 **Ripon Way** housing estate where only 50 per cent of the 4,000 houses had been completed. The 800 building workers decided to **down tools** and hold a protest meeting with their deputations of the different unions, asking for the Council's move to be officially regarded as a **lock-out.**! The L.C.C.'s premature finish to the mammoth building project was a direct result of all the unofficial strikes that had broken out at the beginning of the year and which were said to have been communist-inspired.

At the beginning of the strike, the builders' union steward of the **National Federation of Building Operatives.** and organiser of the protest meeting, told a local newspaper reporter *"We are not afraid and we are proud of what we have done in the past. We will fight any action to close down the job. We cannot afford to let this go by for the sake of the other building projects"*.

Police contingents arrived at the No. 2 site to control any outbreak of trouble from the workers. They were greeted with good humoured cries from isolated pockets of a well organised meeting. After the resolution of taking the matter up with the unions, it was unanimously approved by the men and the meeting dispersed.

The first news of the L.C.C.'s decision was broadcast by posters which appeared on the sites the night before the meeting. No reason was given to workers for the winding up. When the leader of the L.C.C. arrived back in London after a visit to Copenhagen, he confirmed that they were going to close the site. The decision had already been taken by the L.C.C. because the series of unofficial strikes by the building workers had continually disrupted and delayed the building schedule.

He said *"Despite an improvement in the output the position had greatly deteriorated because there had been another unofficial strike and go-slow, which had a serious affect on increasing cost beyond original limits. The Council consequently had no alternative but to carry out its warning to instruct the contractors to suspend the whole project."*

There had been a sharp drop in production since the end of June 1952 despite incentive bonuses offered to improve productivity. The statistics were shown in the contractor's progress report.

The estate's building programme was originally started under a cost-plus contract. This meant that each fresh concession made to the men soared the overall price on the estate. It was probable that work on the estate could be resumed following negotiations which offered the L.C.C. the opportunity of an entirely new contracting basis and employment of a new labour force. Until then Boreham Wood would be crippled by stalemate.

With only three days to go before the closing down of the Ripon Way estate, the L.C.C.'s biggest housing estate, an all-out drive was made to complete 50 houses before the wages were paid out for the last time to the 1,250 building workers on the site.

In an interview the chief surveyor of the 600 acre site said they were going all-out to complete between 50 and 60 houses before the contract ended. One of the houses was needed for a midwife. The tenants of 727 occupied houses had a residents' doctor and a minister, but still needed a midwife.

As the frames of the selected houses began to swarm with workers directed from elsewhere on the estate, the other workers began the sad job of throwing tarpaulins over the roofless homes which were to be left uncompleted. Falling over the buildings one by one, the tarpaulins, which gave protection to the derelict homes against the elements of an approaching winter, seemed like shrouds for the project that was meant to give homes and a new town to 4,000 families in great need of better living conditions.

In September 1952 it was very good news, at last, for everyone because Boreham Wood's new town had been reprieved! The L.C.C. had withdrawn its closure notice so the men could go back to work. They hoped to finish the £7,000,000 project as speedily as possible. There had been too much time and far too much money lost.

Was it really necessary? What were the full facts of this whole miserable business? And what happened next?

The workers' complaints were mainly against the contractor, Gee, Walker and Slater Ltd. but the root of the trouble had been the number of agitators among the men.

The L.C.C. retained the contractor against whom all the complaints had been directed, and who kept the same labour force complete with its agitators. One of the things asked for by the building workers during ructions was for the L.C.C. to take control of the building. The other was that an enquiry should be held into the whole business.

The enquiry was granted and until its report became available they could only guess at Boreham Wood's future. It was thought that perhaps one result would be for the contractors to be paid off so another contractor could be appointed to complete the outstanding building work.

The L.C.C. were placed into a very serious financial position where they could not allow the work to drag out any longer. The men had to realise that their future lay in their own cooperation. Since the start of the project labour disputes had added over £100,000 to the planned cost.

It appeared that the men, at the slightest provocation, downed tools or went slow and had no thought or consideration for what affect this could have on the homes for the homeless. The builders' steward said that it was unfair to blame the men for the additional costs. He accused the contractors of bad administration, a charge which they denied. One of the contractor's executives described the accusation as **untrue**. He claimed that all the trouble had been caused by the strikes and *go-slows*, none of which involved union principles.

That is where the answer lay in this whole business. None of the strikes appeared to have involved union principles. They were unofficial and illegal because the union stewards had been taking the law into their own hands and as a result had caused much trouble, loss of time and had cost tax-payers a lot of money.

The L.C.C. was fully aware of the facts and it was only after an assurance from the men that they would consult the regional officials before taking any action that the L.C.C. withdrew its decision to close the contract.

It was hoped that the men had got it into their heads that the proper way to go about settling their disputes was through legal union action, and that the *National Federation of Building Trade Operatives* would conclude that their stewards on the site had been wielding too much power, and should curb their representatives' enthusiasm a little.

It was also said that a building site was not the place for proving communist or any other principles. It was a place for building houses. This was the final advice to the men whose records show the building of only 727 houses in two and a half years.

It was recommended that the L.C.C. be better advised before jumping to conclusions that the only way out was by closing contracts and should consider the opinions of the men who have to do the job.

The contractors were advised that when they were involved in anything of vital importance to many thousands of people they should cooperate a little more with the Press. Then the people would understand more fully their point of view, too!

In November 1952, after a series of decisions, retractions and compromises arising from the labour dissatisfactions of the Ripon Way L.C.C. Estate, in Boreham Wood, the private commission specially set up by the London County Council to investigate whether the £7,000,000 project was still feasible in view rising costs brought in a favourable verdict.

The 600 acre site starring the district was to be pushed on to its conclusion as a prompt answer to London's homeless overflow population.

When the Commission's report was laid before the *General Purposes Committee of the L.C.C.* it listed conclusive reasons which left no doubt about the importance of the undertaking as the satellite town of London Region's outer perimeter development.

The Commission had been up in early September following the L.C.C.'s action on August 22nd, in erecting closure notices on the No.1 and No.2 sites of the estate. The reasons put forward for the decision at the time were that the unofficial strikes and go-slow tactics on the part of the 1000 building workers sent up costs to a prohibitive level.

The decision came when only 2,000 of the planned 4,000 houses had been completed. The closure notices were posted four days later and 800 building workers gathered on the No.2 Site in a resentful protest meeting against what they termed as a *lock-out*. The outcome of the protest meeting was an appeal to the various building unions involved. This led to a temporary withdrawal of the ban, following the urging of the unions. It was during this lull in negotiations that the Commission was called to report on the situation and its immediate prospects.

The members were the leader of the L.C.C., the Chairman of the General Purposes Committee and the Chairman of the Housing Committee who were the three chief L.C.C. policy makers.

The Commission expressed strong disapproval of the tactics employed by the shop stewards on the job including their need to anger the contractors.

A point specially stipulated in the Commission's report was that the men should use the official machinery within the building industry for settling future disputes and not take unethical action to stop work over trivial grievances. The crux of the misunderstandings which made the site's past so noteworthy had been overcome. A labour relations officer was appointed to directly mediate in any other problems in Boreham Wood.

A sign of the fresh life which blew through Ripon Way was the increased output of between 20 and 25 houses a week compared with eight recorded during the dispute.

Continuing into November 1952 it was revealed that another demonstration was planned by building workers. This demonstration could have swung the balance against the Commission's conclusions. It included a march of all the workers along the length of Ripon Way to Theobald Street. Undoubtedly the Commission might have seen fit to reverse its favourable decision and called for either a change of the present contractors, Messrs. Gee, Walker and Slater Ltd., or the entire cessation of work.

It was understood that the demonstration was called as a protest against the dismissal of 240 workers employed by Messrs. Terson's Ltd., the building contractors of Putney Heath. Among the charges levelled against Terson's were allegations that the firm were employing *black labour* and forcing out 40 union members.

Union stewards from the firm, visiting the No. 2 Site in Ripon Way, appealed to 300 workers for financial assistance for the workers in the dispute. But a more forcible action was urged upon the meeting and the decision was made to march from Ripon Way to Theobald Street, via Shenley Road and the meeting called for a similar motion from 500 other workers on the *No.1 Site* in Theobald Street. The march was already to go, just eight days before the Commission's conclusions but then the march was inexplicably called off!

The L.C.C., Messrs. Gee, Walker and Slater and the unions involved were all bound to secrecy from expressing the real turbulent state of the No.1 and No.2 Sites. No statements were issued to the Press. Shrouded with secrecy the only evidence of the *behind the scenes drama* was given out by the workers themselves, who were nonplussed by the directive to first march and then countermanding the order which averted a momentous Boreham Wood crisis.

An intimation that the action was more serious than the demonstration and was in fact an organised strike was illustrated when a casual labourer, when applying for a job on the L.C.C. Estate was tersely told: *"Sorry, there's no more employment, we are on the verge of a strike!"*

Although the protest march was called off for no apparent reason, it is obvious that after a weekend of reflection the organisers realised the true gravity of the step which would have put the L.C.C.'s most ambitious project back into a mire of controversy and dispute.

In December 1952, there was yet another strike, and this time it was very serious. All 750 men stopped work on the No.2 Ripon Way site. The contractors then issued them with an ultimatum to return to work or the job closes! The dispute was over the dismissal of their former chief site steward of the National Federation of Building Trade Operatives and eight other union stewards.

The £7,000,000 housing project earned itself the title of *"The L.C.C.'s Outer London Perimeter epitaph!"*

The men, all employed on the No.1 and No.2 Sites, stopped work against a bleak backcloth of 1,500 unfinished houses. They were told that the union credentials of their chief union steward had been withdrawn. When he and the other stewards suspended their work within working hours to discuss the issue and refused a foreman's order to resume work, they were all summarily dismissed.

At a meeting, which lasted for three hours, there had been some intensive discussion and all reporters were barred. A statement was issued later by the chief union steward, it ran

"So far as the men on the job are concerned, we have had a meeting and have decided to stay out. We have discussed the position and have decided to stand our stewards until they are reinstated. The employers have victimised the representatives."

But the resolution behind the statement was not unanimous. At a meeting to which the local press were admitted, resolutions being passed by speakers were frequently interrupted by cries of *"But were the stewards in the right? More facts please....and What's the case again?"*

At the meeting the popular vote brought the 750 workers of both sites back on the job, pending a decision between the management and the workers delegation. After the resolution was passed a terse telephone message received from the L.C.C.'s chairman was read out aloud. The message was addressed to the union regional secretary, it ran *"Will you please inform the strike committee that unless the men return to work the job will close the next day."*

The whole estate was still turbulent and dissatisfied with the union, contractor and L.C.C.'s actions which had brought the 2-year disputes history of the Boreham Wood Estate, up to a total of 17 unofficial strikes and 22 go-slows.

Two hours deliberation at the **Disputes Commission** meeting failed to reach a decision. They decided that the Secretary of the **London Master Builders Association** should meet the Secretary of the **London Region of the National Federation of Building Trade Operatives**. They reported the case and their findings to the National Secretaries. If the Party lodged an appeal, the case would be heard by a National Council.

It has been extremely difficult to establish exactly when all these building disputes actually ended, but it was sometime in 1953. I have searched all the local newspaper archives to see if there were any news or headlines relating to the ending of the disputes, but nothing was reported! At the end of the day everyone went back to work and the L.C.C Council Houses programme was finally completed.

Before this programme was started the land on which they built the No.1 and No.2 L.C.C. housing estates was still fields and farmland. Other new houses in Boreham Wood were built by the contractors John Laing for the Elstree Rural District Council. John Laing were later commissioned to build other houses in Boreham Wood and the Manor Way parade of shops. They were also involved with the building of new factories in the area. There were already some factories that occupied the land; these were built sometime in the 1930s and 1940s.

My detailed street plan in Fig 11. shows the development at the No.2 L.C.C. Housing Estate where they built many different styles of houses, flats and bungalows.

Schools

When we first moved to Boreham Wood there were few schools. While we were waiting for more to be built, we had to travel by coach to a temporary school called *High Canons* in Well End.

My third school, *Saffron Green*, hadn't even been built; in fact the site that was chosen for its construction was still an empty field directly opposite where we lived and was situated right along side the A1 Barnet By-Pass; commonly known as the Great North Road.

In the 1950s, after housing, a high priority for the growing population of Boreham Wood was to build more schools. There were already some, including *Furzehill School* built in 1912 and *Hillside Secondary Modern School*, built in 1939, which incidentally, first opened and closed its doors the day after war broke out.

It was calculated that these schools would not be big enough to cope with the huge increase in the additional numbers of people and families coming to the town.

This critical educational situation in Boreham Wood caused the Hertfordshire County Council to ask the Ministry of Education to approve the building of more schools to accommodate all the children on the new L.C.C. housing estates to avoid the fast growth of Boreham Wood causing a big educational problem.

The Ministry of Education told the Elstree Rural District Council that, however desirable it may be to build more schools in Boreham Wood, it had the needs for Hertfordshire and the country as a whole to consider.

At the time it was recommended that they should build some mixed infants and junior schools, a secondary and a modern grammar school to meet the increasing school demands of the community and that these should be included in their building programme. A list of 16 primary and secondary schools proposals was sent to the Ministry for Education's approval; this was for the county's 1954 -1955 building programme, but many of these proposals had been previously postponed by the Ministry.

The Hertfordshire Education Committee warned the Ministry of Education that further postponement of their building programme would acutely embarrass the County Council and open the way to serious criticism of Hertfordshire's educational facilities. The education officer assured the members that a more comprehensive and detailed report had been sent to the Ministry explaining the county's serious position and pointed out that they were not the maximum requirements; they were the minimum requirements and they should not be cut.

During that period many representations were made to the Ministry of Education and eventually there seemed to be some hope of a capital sum being available in 1951. If consent was not given, a report by the Education Committee stated the situation was so grave, that a special meeting of the committee may be necessary to consider the matter. Information at the time stated that by the end of 1952, it was expected that there would be 600 more secondary modern pupils in Boreham Wood and by 1953, 900 and by 1954, 1200, because of the growth of the L.C.C. housing estate.

The Boreham Wood school situation became so serious that children had to be taught in canteens and staff rooms. The situation would get worse because of the very large numbers of children already in the area and the rate at which they were still coming into the district.

This was setting the local and county education authorities a pressing problem.

There was a lot of *to-ing and fro-ing* by the pupils in different buildings as the need demanded; they were sent to makeshift schools such as High Canons, the Church Hall in Manor Way and even the Village Hall in Shenley Road.

In November 1952 the Hertfordshire Education Committee recommended the approval of sketch plans and schedule for Saffron Green Primary School to be built. This was to be a new junior, mixed infants' school and health clinic, all on the same site.

The County Council was asked to approve a capital vote of £57,361 for the school, for which the total annual expenditure, including teachers' salaries, was expected to be £10,000.

In the same year the Ministry for Education finally gave the approval for the building of Saffron Green School and said that it would be ready by Easter 1954. In 1953-1954 they approved the building of an additional Secondary Modern School, Infant School and a Grammar School to be built in 1954.

In October 1952 a temporary solution to the problem of lack of school accommodation at Boreham Wood was proposed. A large mansion in Well End, known as High Canons, which had been used as a private boarding school, could be adapted to provide extra classes and to relieve the overcrowding in schools.

Later it was announced that the Education Committee had sanctioned the use of High Canons, as an additional school accommodation for Boreham Wood.

High Canons was the property of the Hertfordshire County Council and it was estimated that the school accommodation could be provided in its spacious rooms for about 200 children. The scheme was outlined at a meeting of the St. Albans Divisional Education Executive when the Primary Sub-Committee said that only slight alterations to the property would be needed.

High Canons was chosen as a temporary solution and accommodation for the children of Boreham Wood from the L.C.C. housing estates and it was said that, as and when they arrive, transport would be provided to ferry them there and back for as long as necessary.

The proposal to take over High Canons was an excellent idea because the lack of school places had not only given concern to parents but the inhabitants of Boreham Wood generally.

New teachers had to be recruited and sent at first to High Canons, and as soon as the new schools were completed to accommodate the new pupils, the teachers would then be transferred to these new schools. The appointment of nine more teachers in addition to the 30 already approved to deal with the increased school population in the county was approved by the Hertfordshire Education Committee. Of the nine extra teachers, two were appointed to High Canons, where 200 children were on the register. Four teachers had previously been appointed to the school, where there were six classes.

Referring to High Canons, it was said that when it was taken over, there would be places for the new children of Boreham Wood. The furniture was available and it was only a question of appointing the staff who could start straight away.

A report at the time stated that High Canons could accommodate the children and repairs, estimated at £300, would be necessary. Some cloakroom additions would need to be carried out. There were sufficient kitchen and dining-room facilities to provide meals.

It was also stated that it could be used straight away if the Ministry of Education approval was given, but it would be necessary to arrange for transport for the children from Boreham Wood as the school was two miles away.

At Boreham Wood's only secondary modern school, Hillside, the pupils' attendance was being extended by 180 places, but this would not do much more than diminish the overcrowding that already existed, or would arise within twelve months. By September 1952, the authority would face a real crisis, Hillside School would be completely full with at least another 500 children to accommodate.

The suggestion for an extension to Hillside Secondary Modern School was agreed which was estimated to cost £30,000. This was recommended for inclusion in the Hertfordshire Education Committee's 1950s building programme. This proposal was reported at a meeting of the Hertfordshire County Council when the urgency sub-committee was authorised to employ private architects, if necessary, to prepare the plans. The Council Education Officer later confirmed that the Hillside Secondary School programme had been approved and work on the extensions to the building had started.

At the time it was suggested that Boreham Wood could have its own three-form entry grammar school by 1954 – providing the Ministry of Education agreed to Hertfordshire County Council's request for the school to be included in its 1952 building programme. The County Council planned to buy land at the junction of Potters Lane and Cowley Hill for the school, for 630 pupils. The building work would take two years to complete.

After many months, if not years, of arguing and bargaining, the authorities finally came to an agreement satisfying everyone who had been involved with the negotiations, to provide what would be beneficial for the school children of Boreham Wood.

What you have just read was purely based on the schools that I attended in Boreham Wood during the 1950s and is only to be used as an example. However, I would say that these criteria would have applied to many other schools that were being built in the area. Other students of that period no doubt have their own stories to tell about their school days in Boreham Wood.

Other schools were built during that period including the following.

Brookfield Primary	Theobald Street
Cowley Hill Primary	Winstre Road
Kenilworth Primary	Kenilworth Drive
Merydene (now Merryfield Community Primary)	Theobald Street
Monksmead Infants	Hillside Avenue
Parkside Primary	Aycliffe Road
Saffron Green Primary	Nicoll Way
St. Teresa's Primary	Fairway Avenue
Summerswood Primary	Furzehill Road
Woodlands Infants	Alban Crescent
Boreham Wood Grammar	Cowley Hill,
Campions Secondary Modern - demolished	Stapleton Road
Holmshill Secondary Modern	Shenley Road
Lyndhurst Secondary Modern - demolished	Gateshead Road

Campion's School Construction 1955

Fig 147. [E.B.W.M.]

Infants going home in wintry conditions from Campion's School, still a building site
January 1956

Fig 148. [E.B.W.M.]

Employment

During the early 1950s one of the main problems which the L.C.C. housing scheme in Boreham Wood had presented to the authorities was the provision of local employment for the future residents. It was expected that there would be numerous applications to build on the L.C.C. estates by the A1. Barnet-Bye-Pass.

At the time some proposals were made to build around 50 factories in Boreham Wood which would employ about six thousand people. Judging by the number of factories being erected during a period of six years it appeared that there would definitely be no labour surplus in Boreham Wood.

It was estimated that an average of ten factories a year could be built and that these would provide a choice of a variety of employment for approximately 6,000 wage earners who were expected on the new L.C.C. housing estates.

Here are some examples of the factories that were around in the 1950s. The first factory, SE Opperman was a local engineering company who, in the 1940s, specialised in making gearboxes. Between 1956 and 1959 they designed and produced an inexpensive family saloon called the *Unicar*. During this period the company produced around 200 cars.

The 'Unicar' built by
SE Oppermans
1956

Fig 149. [E.B.W.M.]

It was a lightweight three-wheel vehicle with a fibre-glass body which sold for around £399.10s.0d (£339.50p). The car offered little in the way of comfort, having canvas, deck-like seats, but it was economical to run. The car had a top speed of 60mph and went through some rigorous road tests when it was taken to some mountains in Wales. One of their employees, who was involved with the road trials, said that he would never do it again! Sadly, in 1959 and due to the introduction of the Mini, it signalled the end for the Unicar.

During my research, I was able to ask Phoebe, one of our original neighbours in Knebworth Path, if she remembered anything about Opperman's and much to my surprise, she said that she had once worked there as a wages clerk from 1955 to 1959.

She also confirms that my father worked there at the same time, but she couldn't remember exactly what he did. She said that he was always walking about with a piece of paper in his hand, trying to look as if he was working!

The A1 Barnet-Bye Pass looking south towards Stirling Corner, in the distance to the right the clock tower of SE Oppermans. The round fronted shaped building with masts is the Royal National Life Boat Depot.
c1950

Fig 150. [D.A.]

Next to this factory we had the supply and repair depot for the R.N.L.I (Royal National Life Boat Institution). This site was chosen because of its excellent facilities for road and rail connections between the South and East Coasts.

The depot was open twenty-four hours a day, seven days a week and could supply spare parts to any life boat stations around the coasts of Britain and Ireland with a minimum of delay.

During this time, six factories were already well under construction on the John Laing estate in the Elstree Way which would employ approximately 760 people; considerably reducing the number of people moving into the area who would be unable to find work.

These new factories would provide a variety of employment: the Associated Transfer Company Ltd started in December 1949 would employ about forty people; the Gorta Engineering Co. Ltd started in 1950 in Chester Road would employ fifteen people; the Leyland Motor Company started in Warwick Road in March 1950, would employ about another ninety people.

The largest of the new factories was the Adhesive Tapes Co. Ltd., which was built in the Elstree Way. The foundation stone for this £400,000 factory was laid in the month of June 1950 and marked another milestone for the industrial development of Boreham Wood. This factory has long since gone and has been replaced with modern offices and warehouses.

The factory, when completed in 1951, employed about a 1000 workers and was one of several factories that were under construction in the Elstree Way.

Keeping pace with the rapid industrial development of the area was the Elstree Rural District Council which had had a proud record of being among the most progressive housing authorities in the County.

One of the firms , no longer in Boreham Wood, that was advertising in 1952 was Bullens in the Elstree Way.

The Bullens organisation provided services to industry, including export packing and shipping, door-to-door trailer service and the continent, office and factory removals and commercial storage and distribution. At the time this firm had over 400 employees throughout its various Branches in the U.K.

Built in the 1930s
the original front entrance for
Elliott Brothers (London) Ltd
in Elstree Way
2009.

Fig 151. [V.R.]

The front and side entrance of
Wanson's
Elstree Way
2009.

Fig 152. [V.R.]

Typical 1930s and 1950s
Industrial Fronts in the Elstree Way
2009

Fig 153. [V.R.]

This concludes my account of 1950s as I was growing up in Boreham Wood. It was then a small township in contrast with its place in today's Hertsmere .

INDEX

Occasional Paper No.4

March 2012

*E*lstree and

*B*oreham

*W*ood

*M*useum

Our Village Hall, Shenley Road

1926-2011

Peter Stokes

Cover

Photograph of the Village Hall

Borehamwood 1960's

Contents	Page
Historic Background	3
The WW2 Years	7
Post WW2	8
Other Community Halls	11

Published by Elstree and Borehamwood Museum 2010

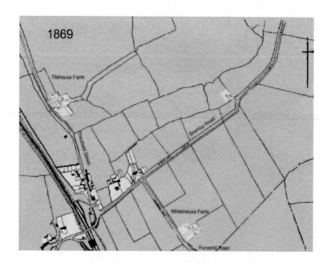

Borehamwood in 1869

Our Village Hall, Shenley Road. 1926-2011.
Historic Background

The 'Village Hall' known as the Church Hall, was opened next to All Saints Parish Church on Friday the second of February 1926. The vicar the Rev. H.F.G Curgenven, introduced Mrs Emily Wellington, wife of local benefactor Mr James Booker Blakemore Wellington, she declared to the well wishers present, the New Hall next to the Parish Church of All Saints, was now open.

The following afternoon a whist drive took place followed by a public dance with the 'Pogo' orchestra of banjo, piano, violin and cello. On Sunday the hall was admired by worshippers and welcomed for use by the Sunday school.

Thus began an extension of the social life of the growing village of Borehamwood, to the east of the hamlet of Theobald Street, created by population growth to 2000 locally, this continued because Elstree railway Station made commuting more popular.

1920's Pogo Band

The township was now maturing after World War 1, with an industrialised commercial character, and the reduction of agricultural activity.

Community social centres around the village and parish had grown with the churches - the way of the world in the post Victorian era.

Secular groups would be a thing of the future, meeting in public halls, with the middle classes entertaining their friends at home.

Meeting Halls were used by other churches, the Methodist church in Shenley used the hall of the former work house. The Congregationalists, a building on the east side of Elstree High Street, no longer used as a Church. The Baptists first met in the parlour of Oak Cottage, Theobald Street. Their Church, still in its original position, is now a florist shop, opposite the railway station in Station Road, the former Gasworks Lane. A mission hall was connected to the Parish Church of St.Nicholas, also in Theobald Street, known as 'The Church of the Good Shepherd' it was modelled on the Salvation Army.

The unfinished All Saints Church had existed as the Chancel with it's High Altar, flanked to the west by a hut-like structure serving as it's Nave when used on Sundays. Completed in 1910, it was dedicated and recognised as the new Parish Church.

All Saints Parish Church in Borehamwood was predated by the mission hall in Theobald street, associated with the Parish church of St Nicholas in Elstree .

The Wellington and Ward photographic factory in Shenley Road had a social hall (known as the Dufay Hall when that firm had the premises.) The building was made of prefabricated corrugated iron, replicated in the revered 'Village Hall' built next to the Church in the 1920s, the era of 'Tin Tabernacles' made of this metal, which resisted bending.

Local parish life through the first world war reflected national life, with church membership at 33% of the population and a raised community spirit, with the new large Parish Church, for worship.

Post war growth was in evidence, All Saints Church had a plot of land for community development in Shenley road. In 1917 a new vicar, the Reverend Curgenven was welcomed, well supported by the effective Parish Council. Something of a rivalry was detected between the old and new parishes.

J.B.B.Wellington, managing director of Wellington and Ward, with his wife Emily, were believed to have been piqued by their marginal acceptance in the mildly feudal Elstree Village, as they represented commerce and industry. This reinforced their benevolence toward 'All Saints'.

George Walton a Glasgow architect of distinction had designed their home, 'The Leys', (now a nursing home) in Barnet Lane. He prepared an impressive, practical proposal for a Parish Hall, the drawing for which is still extant. In brick, double fronted with a mansard roof in the style of a residence. The entrance hall, flanked by two classrooms had a billiard room above. To the rear, a pitched roofed hall with a performance stage and seating for some 300 people. A building of substance and style.

Fund raising began from 1920 with £200, proceeds from two bazaars this set expectations. By 1925 aspirations were satisfied by the planning of a corrugated 'iron hall' on the model of the 'Wellington/Dufay' Hall, once situated in what is now the Town's major shopping mall.

Messrs Boulton and Paul of Norwich were approached. As civil engineers they had and still have a wide product range. They built a large proportion of 'Sopwith Camel' airframes in the war years, in 1925 they specialised in prefabricated corrugated iron buildings for rail delivery across the country. The construction system made possible completion of our, later revered Hall, by the end of the year, at the cost of £2230.

Drawing of the new Church Hall by Alan Lawrence

When it opened the facility was the largest public hall in the district, it could accommodate some 150 people. Enthusiastically taken up by the community with both parish and secular bookings, fulfilling diverse social needs. The National model of the village hall allied with the parish church, a centre of community close to the shops and pubs.

In that decade, as the family centred universal day of rest and relaxation Sunday was observed in church going families, including Sunday school for the young, with infant and junior levels, as a model of respectable behaviour, potential belief, and a break for parents in responsibility.

By 1934 the Rev W. Maddock was the incumbent of All Saints and he brought an element of fresh thinking to the parish, two disparate concerns. He learned that the hall next to the Church, was not, in practise always available to meet Church requirements, and while the founding mission hall in Theobald Street, was in the ownership of the church, its primary use was as a men's club with something of a warring relationship with the leaseholders in terms of its purpose, facilities, sobriety and maintenance.

By 1936 arrangements were completed for the erection behind 'The Village Hall' of the new brick built 'Sunday School Hall' financed by the sale of the mission hall and two cottages as funding, together with generous donations from church people.

Sunday School Hall

The complex of All Saints church and its two halls served as centre of the community, as housing and shopping premises expanded into former farm land. In this the emergent industry was film making. Actors and studio personnel arrived at Elstree railway station, other studio workers lived locally, this may have stamped the image of 'Elstree' on the studios.

The emergent town and the village hall served as settings in film making, business expanded in the community, a proportion of the studio principals took up residence. Press reporting of the era covered aspects of interest, incidentally waking civic responsibility for fire services with the presence of films and film making. A village hall entertainment in support of Fire Brigades was organised by J, Grossman of British International Picture Studios, supported by Famous Film Stars, one was Seymour Hicks of drama fame.

In the late 30's, there was thought of the development of the town with a Garden City image complementing Elstree Film Studios. The enterprising developers Messrs Laings had constructed the Middlesex County Hospital at Shenley with Royal approval in 1934, the firm bought land to the east of the growing town, south of Elstree Way, connected with the new Barnet By-Pass.

This became the first coherent housing development, Laings Elstree Estate. Work proceeded enthusiastically with roads and soundly built quality houses, of fairly low density. The range was named – 'Elsland', 'Elsdale', 'Elsbury', and 'Elsonia' etc. The enterprise appeared set fair, complimented in the west with intent to extend the L.P.T.B. underground system to Elstree and the Aldenham maintenance facility.

The WW2 Years
In September 1939 the second world war began, lasting till May 1945. A time of international conflict, with the civilian population fully engaged accentuated by war in the air. In retrospect, social change was notably seen in this area.

After the Munich crisis of 1938, the organisation for Air Raid Precautions, emerged, later recognised as Civil Defence. From the start to the end of the war the village hall, because of the central position, was requisitioned for government use. In the early war years it was an A.R.P. Post and ambulance station, also used in liaison with Police and Fire Services and local Hospitals, and with public utilities for water, gas and electricity.

Civil Defence

The film studios in their 'Elstree' persona virtually shut down during the war years, these and local factories deployed their resources in support of the Aircraft manufacturers De Havilland and Handley Page, at Aldenham and to the north of Radlett and Hatfield. Local people took up this employment and the population was augmented locally by the Nation's and allies armed forces.

In the later years of the war, from 1943 the Village Hall did service as a 'British Restaurant' run by the government at subsidised rates, providing lunchtime meals, (ration book free) for one shilling. It was estimated that 3oo meals a day could be served, to factory workers, business people, and residents. This foreshadowed the present shop trade in Shenley road.

Along with these activities, on Saturday afternoons transformation of the Hall was achieved for evening dances. A welcome social event for Servicemen and women based in the area mixing with local people.

Post WW2
At the end of the war, the hall remained requisitioned until November 1946. A notice appeared in formal tones, 'After being out of our control since September 1939, the church hall has been de-requisitioned. Much needs to be done to put it in condition for general use. It will be done as quickly as possible in order that the many who want to hire it can be met. Trustees will soon be ready to elect a caretaker'.

Things then proceeded to normality, with various occasions reported, wedding receptions, social meetings, performances of the Osbourne Players related to

Borehamwood Football Club, amalgamated in 1948 by combining the Borehamwood Swifts and Royal Retournez, formalised in the Village Hall which was used for winter indoor training! Elstree Civil Defence group was still active and was involved with the Dick Whittington pantomime of 1949, featuring many local names as players and in the dance troupe.

In the 1950s a report on the two Halls showed the diversity in the use of both the Village Hall and the Sunday school hall.

(a) Church related, Sunday school classes, Passion plays, Kings Messenger meetings, Mothers Union, W.I. meetings, Whist Drives, Easter and Christmas bazaars, The May Festival, Scouts and Guides, Jumble sales, All Saints fellowship, Old Time Dances, Church Lads Brigade, Sunday school parties etc.

(b) Separately listed as non Church related were Dances, Societies annual general meetings, local Drama club, plays, film shows, exhibitions, club meetings, bazaars, cage bird shows, garden show, whist drives, annual dinners, talks, concerts etc.
An interesting record of diversity. In retrospect it could be seen as an atypical adjunct to community life.

The town now entered a time of rapid population growth, well along the predicted growth curve on policy for rehousing from the London overspill and the national growth in population. Regrettably no 'New Town' social planning was enacted, unlike the eve of war Laing initiative. The Village culture just grew around the major shopping centre and the Parish Church and Village Hall.

Press reports , and the Parish magazine, reported local activities and happenings such as The Crowning of the May Queen. Attempts to involve 'the Londoners' from the new estates, in this country style event, met with failure. The event was returned to All Saints. The summer fair event was not offered a local residents garden of a suitable size, so would be held in the Church grounds and the Church Hall.

Sunday school outings continued to be centred on visiting coastal resorts by train from Elstree station as it was still named. The floor of the Sunday school hall was replaced, the men of the congregation stripped out the old Columbian pine, specialist contractors replaced it in Missandra hardwood.

In the late 1950s approximately 400 children attended the Sunday school, the seniors accommodated in the Church and juniors in the Village Hall, the kindergarten met in the Sunday School Hall. As with the national scene, this represented a peak in attendance of Sunday worship by the young.

The church magazine reflects the difficulty in the recruitment of teachers. The decline in Sunday school attendance was recognised as a waning of parental support and motivation.

Sunday School

Undoubtedly, 'Church of England' church going, declined from the 1960s in our locality, reflecting social change broadened thinking and the blandishment of television. Also, nonconformist worship diffused into the whole field of alternative faiths, as shown in a shrinking world emphasising alternatives. All Saints Church with the two halls, was no longer a strong conjoined relationship in the community.

As the centenary of All Saints Church in the world of the new millennium drew near, it continued in good heart with a strong and diverse congregation. The 'Village Hall' still presented its vintage image on the major thoroughfare and the interior decorative appearance remained remarkably high, due to dedicated congregation workers and other well wishers. The smaller complimenting brick Sunday School, sheltered from gaze behind the Church. Whilst both were in the care of separate trustees, circumstances dictated that overall use was mainly secular.

The Sunday School Hall by this time was solely in use on weekdays as a children's crèche and play school.

The local Town, supported by Hertsmere Borough Council and Hertfordshire County Council, recognised that a local town community centre was desirable for Elstree and Borehamwood.

Happily the 'Village Hall' site in its central position was an obvious choice. By October 2008 plans were prepared for the new community hall. This was to be a building of substance, balancing All Saints church itself, rising a storey above nearby shopping premises. The Library was to be accommodated with the inclusion of the Local museum and various meeting halls and rooms.

The ground area covers that of the two previous Church Halls, this land represents the contribution of the church to the County project. All the groups using the Halls were accommodated in other local facilities, the Women's Institute, who met, in the Dufay Hall, prior to the construction of the Village Hall moved conveniently to Allum Hall, for example.

Fittingly the first major celebration of the local interfaith group was one of the last meetings held in the Village Hall in November 2009, using the stage. Also the church congregation's tea party, after celebration of All Saints Church Centenary service. The internal decor sparkled, it's structure and fittings, a throw back to the 1930s, tempting false thoughts of preservation of it as a tribute to the 'Corrugated Tin Tabernacles'

The area is now enclosed, as the intent to proceed, when financial constraints of the unprecedented economic era are relieved. Hopefully this will signal the emergence from doom and gloom, to 'keep calm and carry on' mode.

Other Community Halls
Prior to the 1939-1945 war, Elstree village had no substantial meeting hall, the growing Borehamwood was limited to the Wellington works Social Hall and in wartime the occasional use of the Village Hall, the popular view is that local public houses staged dances and other events, giving younger people and Service personnel stationed locally had opportunities to meet and enjoy life.

As the town expanded and gained its name, Borehamwood, more community halls emerged, associated with new Church building, with others related to the local authority. The Village Hall was matched by others of a similar size. Two others at opposite ends of the Town's main road were of note.

The manor House in Allum Lane was bought by public subscription in 1951 by a community association, an initiative independent of local authority funding, this possibly might appear to be a return to the separate areas of Elstree and Borehamwood.

By 1953 the community centre expanded. In the grounds stood an excellent Hall, semi circular in style, a pleasing concrete structure mindful of an enlarged military Nissan hut. It incorporated a well equipped stage at one end, at the other, a first floor with catering facilities. Complementing the various facilities in the house, it became Allum Hall, a centre for the community of the town.

Circa 1971 next to the Civic offices, Maxwell Hall appeared, thought to be the initiative of local businessman, Ivor Bailey of the B.S.P. drafting firm. Primarily devoted to youth interests, it has continued very successfully.

The current Hertsmere Borough listing of seating: Aberford park hall 120. All Saints Church Hall 130, Allum Hall 470,(non smoking being stressed) Bellhaven Court Hall 70, Borehamwood Football Club 180, Fairway Hall 80 to 100, Farriers Way Hall 80, Maxwell Park Community Centre 150, The Three Ways Community Centre 200. The list covers those for lettings and excludes others matched to their local community needs, such as Organ Hall Community and other various Churches.

This document centres on key and various aspects of local history and continues in that vein, haunted by what might have been...

The expanding population of the town needed a large centre for public use and entertainment, this was identified by the Elstree Rural District Council in 1959, when plans for a public hall and swimming pool were drafted.

In 1962 this scheme was deferred to concentrate on the swimming pool. At that time there was a plan to transport those with swimming ambitions, by bus to the open air pool in Finchley, North London, this was at a minimal charge to participants and proved popular. This outlook echoes that which placed the technical support centre for the National Lifeboat Organization here in Borehamwood.

In November 1970 the rural District Council proceeded with building a hall between the swimming pool and the County library. In April 1971 architects were appointed, this gave interested residents the opportunity to be bussed as a group, to facilities of different types around outer North London, for their opinions to be validated. In June 1972 building work started to the hopeful satisfaction of all.

By 1974 it was in use. With the capacity of 700 people for performances, it accommodated 450 for dances and 300 for dining. A multi purpose hall, it could be used for stage performances for music, drama, ballet and Variety, as well as film shows. Other activities were meetings, lectures, debates, educational activities, boxing and wrestling, flower shows, exhibitions and conferences with catering facilities. A lounge area was available for wedding receptions etc, when the main hall was not in use. The stage had excellent facilities, dressing and green rooms, and a scenery dock. An unsung feature was chair storage area in the building with uncluttered space in all other areas.

It fulfilled all its purposes very well, and was an asset to the town and the area for the seventeen years or so. Allowing my personal recollection of particular satisfaction, in that it encouraged development of local music societies in the performing arts. A number of groups grew and flourished, with their own supporters and audiences, in addition to growth of the professional theatre.

Our local operatic society worked in the halls, opening with 'Pirates of Penzance' through to 'Sound of Music' on the eve of its closure in 1991. The local press was enthusiastic over the years, reporting Hertsmere Centre events specifically, and of Hertsmere Operatic 'The Society really did us proud'

1990, portents of closure appeared in the local press, correspondence between the new Conservative leader of Hertsmere Borough, and the Town Mayor was reported in the local press. Hertsmere reported a loss of £250,000 a year. In contention with Borehamwood it evidently offered the town council a 99 year lease of the building at peppercorn rent. A press report 'if the town council really believes it to be vital to preserve the Hertsmere Centre, then I suggest you take it over - If you do not accept this proposal then the residents of Elstree and Borehamwood will realise that your determination to preserve the Hertsmere Centre is so much hypocrisy.'

The Hertsmere Centre closed, whether due to ineptitude in marketing or an ambition too far in concept, we do not know. In 1986 the new Council offices for Elstree and Borehamwood Town, with Fairway Hall, had been opened. This small hall served the town well, its site in the   vicinity of the Hertsmere Borough offices, separate and distinct.

As the years moved on, the loss of the Hertsmere Centre continued to rankle. In 1998 a revised complex at its former site next the swimming pool was initiated with a smaller multi purpose theatre. Foundations were laid in 1999.

This was abandoned with a Conservative council replacing Labour, advising that the 500 seat theatre would lose £835,000 a year, backed by a consultant's estimate at £525,000 - the press reported Labours claim that with the termination 73 contractors had been paid off, and equipment destroyed, representing a loss of £8m.

In 2001 a greatly expanded public hall was opened at Allum Hall replacing its former performing hall, whilst a stage is incorporated it faces a flat hall area. It lacks facilities for theatrical productions. In general use it is a great success.

Once again the desire for a local theatre came to the fore from 2005 and plans came to fruition with a grand opening of a 200 seat well equipped facility on the premises of Hertswood Secondary School in 2008. The 'Ark Theatre' was planned as a logical solution, combining the needs of education and local entertainment with the enthusiasm of the Head of drama in administration.

The first public performance by a local society was in March 2009. Problems subsequently, are that whilst the schools needs have been met handsomely, use by others has been inhibited by other factors. Hire charges compare badly, favouring economic use of the Radlett Centre Theatre. This alternative Hertsmere Borough facility has enjoyed an altogether happier history with council support, building an excellent client and customer base for enjoyed performances.

Another major inhibition at the 'Ark' is that only limited parking is allowed on the school site, the pleasure of attending performances is tested by having to walk from the car park near the Civic offices. Someone will doubtless solve the problem. From April 2011 a professional Theatre Manager will hopefully bring a successful outlook for the future.

All the historic activity described in this paper on our old Village Hall with the fullness of time, will blend into the development of the new Community Centre next to All Saints Church.